Reveal the Real

From the editors of

all about **YOU!**

AND **Teen**

Reveal the Real

This edition published in 2002.

Teen and All About You are trademarks of Petersen Publishing Company, L.L.C., and are used with permission. Copyright © 1998 Petersen Publishing Company, L.L.C. All Rights Reserved.

Distributed under license from Petersen Publishing Company, L.L.C.

Published by Troll Communications L.L.C.

Printed in Canada.

10   9   8

Acknowledgments

Special thanks to Roxanne Camron, Beth Mayall, and all the quiz authors: Maureen Basura, Gayle Cohen, Lia Haberman, Stuart Hazleton, Maggie Keresey, Lori Moore, Valerie Morrison, Julie Taylor, Tamara Tuttle, and Tracy Werth.

Cover credits—*Photography:* Eika Aoshima, Botaish Group. *Makeup:* Wendy Ann Rosen, Cloutier. *Hair:* Petra, Visages Style. *Model:* Marisa Ericson. Twinset by Coolwear. Necklace and ring by Cara Stimmel. All makeup from Maybelline.

Table of Contents

Introduction

Grab a pen and get ready to learn all about the real you!

You will find out how easily you make friends; if you're too nice; how strong your friendships are; whether you're an optimist or a pessimist; if you worry too much, and oh-so much more! How cool is that?

Each quiz is loaded with tips and advice from the experts—so you can truly peek inside your soul.

How Happy Are You?

Is the sunny side of the street your scene? Or does it always seem to rain on your parade? Take our quiz and check out how chipper you are.

1 It's Saturday night, and you've got nothing going on—no date and none of your friends are free. What's your mind-set?

❏ a) Groovy. You rent that flick you've been dying to see, grab some munchies, and settle in for a Blockbuster night.

❏ b) Okay, but after an hour you're feeling restless and wish you'd made plans.

❏ c) Crummy. Seems like you're always stuck hangin' solo.

2 You swore life would be perfecto if that cute guy you've been crushin' on would just ask you out. Well, girlfriend, dreams do come true—he just did! Can you keep your pledge?

❏ a) Maybe—if he turns out to be as cool as you thought.

❏ b) Nah, it'll never last. Crushing on him was more fun than actually getting him.

❏ c) What? You're so delirious, you're deaf.

3 You're starting a new school, and it's your first day of class. You feel:

❏ a) a flood of dread.

❏ b) nervous, but excited.

❏ c) total anticipation. You can't wait to get there!

4 You go to bed dreaming about your big date tomorrow with that Leonardo DiCaprio look-alike, but when you wake up in the morning, you find a zit the size of China has sprouted smack in the middle of your forehead. You:

❏ a) —cough! sniffle!—think you're coming down with something; looks like you may have to reschedule. But you'll have a major bonding session with him on the phone to make up for bailing.

❏ b) consider busting out the scissors and sportin' some new bangs, but opt for slapping on a little coverup and laughing it off. You figure if you can woo him tonight, *with* a zit, you're golden.

❏ c) stick a Band-Aid on your head and lock yourself in your room for the next twenty-four hours.

5 A supercool friend is having a get-together at her house, and the guest list reads like a Who's Who of the popular crowd at your school. What's your party plan?

❏ a) You change your outfit ten times and practice looking bored till you steam up the mirror.

❏ b) You dress with style and a smile—and expect to have a good time.

❑ c) What plan? You bow out, saying you have to baby-sit, since you know you could never have a good time hangin' with that snooty crowd.

6 It's Groundhog Day, boys and girls. And it's been one long, icy winter. What pops into your mind?

❑ a) Life!—cool! It's really spring.

❑ b) You hope this spring isn't as rainy as last year's.

❑ c) That poor groundhog will probably die in a late snowstorm.

7 You're getting ready for a night out, and you find a stain on the sleeve of your favorite sweater. You:

❑ a) end up canceling your plans. Everything you like gets ruined!

❑ b) change into something else but spend a major part of your evening worrying over whether the spot will come clean.

❑ c) wear your second-favorite sweater. *C'est la vie*— it's not like it's a priceless designer original or anything.

8 Last night your term paper sounded like genius, but today you're not so sure. What's your brain saying ten minutes after you turn in the paper?

❑ a) There are a few more ideas you wish you'd included, but, hey, it's still passable.

❑ b) What a moron you are! There are tons of things you forgot to include; you'll be lucky to squeak by with a C.

❑ c) No one can cover every little thing—there was a page limit after all. Besides, you worked really hard and learned a lot while you were at it. You've gotta get at least a B+.

9 Your healthy-eating plan worked—you've lost every last stubborn pound just in time for bathing-suit season. Congratulations! Or not?

❑ a) NOT. You haven't been able to keep weight off before. Why should this time be any different?

❑ b) Yes, but you know your friends will still look better than you.

❑ c) Definitely yes! Now your next goal is to keep it off.

10 Your neighbor's new puppy just got loose and made mincemeat of the school science-fair project you spent the past month slaving over. You know there's no way you can recreate your work by the entry deadline. When friends attempt to console you, you:

❑ a) hold back tears, fake a smile, and say, "Really, I'm fine. It's no big deal."

❑ b) talk it out, being honest about how truly bummed out you're feeling.

❑ c) rage, cry, and wallow in self-pity for at least a week, telling everyone you know about this latest hardship you've had to endure.

Which of the following statements apply to you? Mark all the ones that do.

11

❑ You're open to trying new things.
❑ You laugh a lot when you hang out with friends.
❑ You make time to do things you enjoy even when you're feeling too busy.
❑ You feel proud of yourself at least once a week.
❑ You rarely feel jealous of other people.

12

❑ You seem to have more than your share of bad luck.
❑ Friends ask you what's wrong at least once a week.
❑ You're well-known for being a gossip.
❑ You feel lonely a lot.
❑ You frequently feel like your happiness depends on someone or something else.

SCORING

Add up your score below, and then get the scoop on your happiness rating.

1. a) 3	b) 2	c) 1
2. a) 2	b) 1	c) 3
3. a) 1	b) 2	c) 3
4. a) 2	b) 3	c) 1
5. a) 2	b) 3	c) 1
6. a) 3	b) 2	c) 1

7. a) 1	b) 2	c) 3
8. a) 2	b) 1	c) 3
9. a) 1	b) 2	c) 3
10. a) 3	b) 2	c) 1
11. add 3 points for each		
12. subtract 1 point for each		

HAPPY CAMPER   45 TO 32 POINTS

There's not much else for us to say except you're one mighty cheerful mama. You have a positive outlook on life and bounce-back ability when things don't go right. With your optimistic attitude, little setbacks seem like no big deal, and even major mishaps are usually manageable. Our only caution: Be careful not to sugarcoat truly bitter pills. "Being really happy is great. Just make sure you don't avoid facing less-than-happy situations," says Wendy McKenna, a New York psychologist.

HAPPY...MAYBE?   31 TO 18 POINTS

You're a realist. You see life as a mixed bag; you hope for the best but don't actually expect it. Your ability to accept what you get is admirable, but remember that you do have control over your own happiness. Be careful not to put up with problems you could solve or miss out on chances to improve situations that make you unhappy.

"Don't wait for happy things to happen. Create better times yourself," McKenna says. Learn what flips your joy switch—fun times with friends, a hobby you enjoy, or just quiet moments to yourself—then put more of it in your life!

HAPPY...NOT!   17 TO 5 POINTS

Girl, you need to shake that doom-and-gloom 'tude. You may think you're a realist (think again). Or maybe you believe that by anticipating the worst and downplaying the best you'll dodge disappointment. Whatever the reason for your bummage, beware the pessimism: Focus on the dark and you'll never see the light!

"Using happiness to avoid confronting sad feelings isn't realistic—but neither is turning away from happiness," McKenna warns. "It's just self-defeating." Granted, life isn't always a bowl of cherries, but it can't be all bad all the time.

To gain perspective and get a better read on things, McKenna suggests, keep a journal to track your emotions. Write down when you're feeling up and what it is that brings you down. A record of events that upset you may help you realize that things aren't as bad as you think and your happiness is within your control. If you find yourself constantly feeling down, talk to a parent, trusted teacher, or counselor.

DON'T WORRY–BE HAPPY

If stormy weather always seems to blow you off cloud nine, here are a few hints on how to defeat the downers:

•**Know thyself.** Born happy or sunk in sadness? Yes, it's true, you have a partial excuse for that bad mood. Research has found that basic temperament has a big impact on a person's emotional state. In plain old English, this means that if you're upset a lot, it's probably not because your life is tougher than anyone else's—you probably just get upset easier. But don't worry; you're not doomed to a total boo-hoo life. You just need to be extra aware of your emotions to keep from overreacting when things don't go your way.

•**Ditch happiness hang-ups.** Don't think of happiness as a future event or let it depend on things you have no control over. Never say, "I'll be happy when…." Whatever it is you're waiting for, you could have a long wait. Why waste all that time?

•**Expect ups and downs.** Everyone has 'em. It's okay to be down once in a while; just don't dwell on your unhappiness. If you're disappointed with your grade on a test, don't blame yourself or the teacher; learn from your mistakes and move on.

•**Be finicky about friends.** Glum chums can bring you down. Don't forsake a friend in need, but don't let a friend's bad attitude rub off on you either. And if a heart-to-heart leaves you disheartened, buck up with a mood-boosting activity.

•**Raise your EQ (enjoyment quotient).** Seek out fun things to do. Join a club, make plans with friends, do volunteer work. And stay open to new ideas—maybe the boxing class that sounds like a dud will be a, uh, knockout.

•**Don't downplay your deeds.** Take pride in yourself and your accomplishments and pat yourself on the back once in a while. Truth is, you rock—why fight it?

Are You a Leader or a follower?

A re you the leader of the pack? Or do you play follow the leader? Being head honcho isn't about bossing people around—it's about taking action, being positive, and knowing how to help and be helped. Take this quiz and find out if you're born to rule or be ruled.

1 The environmental group at school needs some serious help organizing a fund-raiser for a trip to the rain forest. You're not really the tree-hugger type, so you:

❏ a) volunteer to help, but only if they make you an honorary president. You can't do something for nothing, right? Besides, it'll look good on your transcripts.

❏ b) agree to help and offer a plan of action for the group. After all, you have tons of fund-raising tactics stuffed into your head—why not share a few with the granolas?

❏ c) wait until they ask for your help and spare some free time if you have any. If they're so earth-conscious, why can't they just hitchhike?

2 Friday night plans are up in the air, but your friends have made several suggestions about what to do. Unfortunately, you're the only one who wants to hit a midnight-madness sale at the mall.

You:

❏ a) forget about the sale. If your friends won't go with you, you couldn't possibly go to the mall by yourself.

❏ b) take a vote, do what the majority wants to do, and hit the mall with your mom later that night.

❏ c) veto all other suggestions and go with the mall plan. If anyone protests, you throw a tantrum.

3 There's a sit-in in the cafeteria to protest the school's lack of a recycling policy. You:

❏ a) pass out fliers and rally friends to help out. You also make a few phone calls to check out a recycling company that might donate collecting bins.

❏ b) throw yourself into the spotlight when the camera crews and reporters show up. The sit-in needs a good spokesperson, and you nominate yourself.

❏ c) hang out on the fringes of the sit-in and watch the spectacle unfold. It's interesting to see kids get worked up over cans.

4 You've _____ run for student government.

❏ a) never
❏ b) occasionally
❏ c) always

5 When you work on a group project, you usually:

❏ a) take control of the group. You have a clear picture

of how the project should be done, and you tell the group you'll take care of everything.

❏ b) take whatever assignment is left after everyone has chosen a job. The idea of working in a group doesn't thrill you, and you do your work quickly (to get it over with) and grudgingly.

❏ c) discuss the different parts of the project and take a group vote on who'll do what.

6 There's a new kid in school, and she's a little on the strange/loner side. She's sitting alone at a table in the library. You:

❏ a) barrel over to her table, introduce yourself, and tell her she's your new friend.

❏ b) gather a few friends together and head over to her table to welcome her.

❏ c) ignore her until one of your friends introduces you.

7 You're in a park and notice someone throw regular trash into the recycling bin. You:

❏ a) dive into the bin and sort out the mess.

❏ b) yell at the fool, then tell the park attendant about the mix-up.

❏ c) put your garbage in the right container and walk away.

8 Your parents are planning the family summer vacation, and they're having a tough time deciding on a destination. You:

❏ a) demand to go somewhere sunny, near a beach, and make their lives miserable until they agree.

❏ b) let them fight it out. Family vacations are painful no matter where they are, and the folks wouldn't listen to you anyway.

❏ c) rally your siblings to action. All of you agree (for once) on the vacation choice, and you tell your parents the outcome of the sibling vote.

9 When you get dressed in the morning, you put on:

❏ a) something similar to what you saw a friend wear a few days before. That way you know it matches.

❏ b) anything that makes you feel bold, aggressive, and fashionable. You want to make an impact, and your clothes are the first step.

❏ c) a killer outfit that gives you confidence. Nothing flashy, but nothing boring.

10 You raise your hand in class:

❏ a) every time a question is asked, whether you know the answer or not.

❏ b) when you think you know the answer to a question or have something intelligent to say.

❏ c) only when other people have raised their hands and you're sure you know the answer.

11 If you were class president and wanted to change the school dress code, you'd:

❏ a) start a petition, make a list of the changes you wanted made and why, and meet with the principal.

❏ b) ask the principal. If he/she said no, you'd forget about it.

❏ c) organize a massive demonstration and make big demands, so the ending compromise would seem fair.

12 One of your friends is spouting off about how ridiculous the driving age is. You disagree with her opinion, so you:

❏ a) start to re-evaluate your own opinion. She sounds convincing, so she must be right. Right?

❏ b) put on an interested face and pretend you're listening. By the time she's finished, you've outlined in your head 101 reasons why she's wrong—and you share those thoughts with her.

❏ c) listen to all of the points she makes, then share your opinion about the subject. Hopefully some glimmer of your intelligence will rub off on her.

13 Your friends want to ditch the last two classes of the day to stand in line for concert tickets at the mall. You:

❏ a) tell them it's not a good idea to skip and ask your mom to get the tickets for everyone.

❏ b) follow along and pray you don't get caught.

❏ c) find someone to drive everyone to the mall and forge parents' signatures on notes saying it's okay.

14
You get nominated to serve on the Spring Fling committee, so you:

❏ a) get to work. You round up friends and start planning for the best spring dance ever.

❏ b) take over. You have the perfect idea for the dance, and only you can carry it out.

❏ c) whimper and decline the nomination, saying you're too busy to handle the responsibility.

SCORING

Add up your points and then read on to find out your style.

1. a) 1	b) 3	c) 2	8. a) 1	b) 2	c) 3
2. a) 2	b) 3	c) 1	9. a) 2	b) 1	c) 3
3. a) 3	b) 1	c) 2	10. a) 1	b) 3	c) 2
4. a) 2	b) 3	c) 1	11. a) 3	b) 2	c) 1
5. a) 1	b) 2	c) 3	12. a) 2	b) 1	c) 3
6. a) 1	b) 3	c) 2	13. a) 3	b) 2	c) 1
7. a) 3	b) 1	c) 2	14. a) 3	b) 1	c) 2

BORN TO RULE
33 TO 42 POINTS

You're head of the class in this school of fish, and you've got the makings of a natural leader. You know how to accept help from others and tackle problems as part of a group. You're the perfect combination of listener and doer, and that'll take you places in life. "A good leader knows how to work within a group," says Joseph Palmour, founder of the Archon Institute for Leadership Development. "She makes people feel comfortable, but she also knows how to get the job done." You set a great example for others with your solid leadership skills and communication style.

BORN TO BE RULED   24 TO 32 POINTS

You bend, you quiver, you float. You're a jellyfish in the sea of life. You do what you're told to do—nothing more, nothing less. When it comes to action, you flounder around and follow whoever's in charge. But don't worry—not everyone is a natural-born leader. Even though you're uncomfortable taking charge of a situation, there's a place for you on the leadership ladder. "A very important kind of leadership is practiced by the so-called 'follower,'" says Palmour. "It's her job to join in and support the leader. Sometimes she has to remind the leader that everyone is part of the team, and everyone needs to be respected." It's people like you who keep the leaders in line— tell them what you think and offer your support and help. You've got opinions, feelings, and ideas, and it's time to express them. You may not be leading the pack, but you're part of what makes the pack work.

BORN TO BE RUTHLESS   14 TO 23 POINTS

Attack and kill—that's your style. You're a lone shark looking for your next prey. Whether it's a protest, plan, or decision, you go in for the kill. But it's not personal satisfaction or the thrill of helping others that you're after. It's recognition, power, and control. "Leaders are vulnerable to being too aggressive," says Palmour. "They generally need other people to help loosen them up a little. They just need a little reassurance that they don't have to be in charge of everything in order to belong." So loosen up a little. You may rule your world now, but it won't be long before you're overthrown. Be more flexible, less demanding, and open to other ideas. Whether you like it or not, you need the help of others to be a real leader.

Are You Friends for Life?

Are you and your best bud meant to be? Take this quiz together to see if you'll be friends for life. Mark your answers on the left-hand blank line. Your best bud marks hers on the right. Each of you should fill in the quiz from your own point of view. You'll learn how strong you think your friendship is, and whether your bud sees it the same way.

1 Even the best of friends can get on each other's nerves sometimes. When you guys argue, it's about:

___ ___a. silly stuff, like who's cuter—Gavin or Jay-Kay?

___ ___b. which one of you is nicer, smarter, and more popular. You've always been really competitive.

___ ___c. nothing much. You hardly ever argue with your best bud.

2 When your English teacher pairs everyone up for a project, your best bud gets the guy you've been dying to get close to! You:

___ ___a. set your sights elsewhere. No boy is worth fighting over.

___ ___b. start a rumor about your best bud so you can get the guy. All's fair in love and war.

___ ___c. ask your bud if she'll find out how he feels about you.

3 If your best bud overheard some people dissin' you in the girls' bathroom, she'd:

___ ___a. remember what was said and give you the 411 later.

___ ___b. jump to your defense, even if it meant standing up to the nastiest girls in the school.

___ ___c. probably laugh along with them.

4 Your friend decides to try out for the lead in the school play. While you're helping her rehearse, you realize she makes the cast of *Head of the Class* look Emmy Award–winning. You:

___ ___a. encourage her to keep practicing. Even if she tanks, it's the effort that counts.

___ ___b. crack up during her dramatic scene and hope she gets the message.

___ ___c. tell her the brutal truth so she won't embarrass herself onstage.

5 When you and your bud can't decide which movie to see, you usually:

___ ___a. watch your choice.

___ ___b. watch her choice.

___ ___c. find a movie you both want to see.

6 If you played a prank on your bud, she'd probably:

___ ___a. laugh till she cried, then play one right back on you.

___ ___b. get pretty upset; she hates to be the butt of practical jokes.

___ ___c. tell you how rude you are.

7 You just can't seem to shake the blues. The only person who knows how seriously unhappy you are is your best friend. She:

___ ___a. tells your favorite, most trusted teacher how miserable you are 'cause she's worried about you.

___ ___b. keeps the secret to herself and tries to cheer you up.

___ ___c. lets the secret slip when she's out with other friends.

8 You promised your best bud you'd help clean her house before her parents come back from their ten-day Caribbean cruise. You're all set to scrub when another friend calls up with tickets to an Everclear concert. You:

___ ___a. toss the rags and get ready to rock. You'll help out after the concert.

___ ___b. help your bud, but let her know loud and clear how upset you are that she made you miss the show.

___ ___c. know there'll always be another concert and get busy with that grime.

Scoring

Add up your score and find out if your friendship is forever.

1. a) 2	b) 3	c) 1		5. a) 3	b) 1	c) 2
2. a) 1	b) 3	c) 2		6. a) 2	b) 3	c) 1
3. a) 1	b) 2	c) 3		7. a) 2	b) 1	c) 3
4. a) 2	b) 1	c) 3		8. a) 3	b) 1	c) 2

FRIENDS TILL SHE FINDS ANOTHER   8 TO 12 POINTS

You're a good bud, but you're letting this so-called best friend take advantage of you. Real pals should be able to speak their minds without worrying about the other person rejecting them. Your friend will appreciate you even more when you start acting like an equal.

FRIENDS FOR LIFE   13 TO 19 POINTS

Congrats! You win the friends-for-life award. You'll be able to conquer whatever obstacles come your way 'cause this is one friendship that's worth working for. Plus, as close as the two of you are, you haven't forgotten what it means to be you—and your best bud truly appreciates all your unique qualities.

FRIENDS TILL YOU FIND ANOTHER   20 TO 24 POINTS

Your friend knows not to count on you 'cause you'll ditch her if it suits your needs. Keep this up, and you're gonna find yourself sitting home alone. Next time you promise to be there for her, don't let her down! Your friendship will grow much stronger when your best bud realizes you really care.

Carol Weston, author of *Girltalk* and *For Girls Only*, suggests the following tips for building a better friendship:

• Be a great listener. If your bud is confiding in you, wait till she's finished before complaining about your problems.

• Give her space. As long as no one is left out, you're both allowed to have other friends.

• Be proud of her accomplishments. If your bud made the cheerleading team, don't tell her you think they're all airheads.

• Leave her crush alone. There are plenty of other boys out there.

• Keep it in the vault. Never tell her deep, dark secrets—unless she's in danger.

• Show an interest in her life. Keep up with what she's doing by asking how her test went or if her bro is still bothering her.

• Be a comfort. If she blew an audition or has a humongous zit, it's your time to tell her how great she is.

• Don't be envious of her. Concentrate on how much you like your own looks, grades, and relationships.

• Keep in touch. Whether it's summer vacation or she goes to another school, send your friend e-mail or snail mail, or call her up.

• Don't be an on-again, off-again friend. Always make time for your best bud.

Does Your Bedroom Need a Makeover?

Your clothes definitely make a fashion statement, but have you ever thought about the message your surroundings send?

Check the answers that sound like you.

1 Your room looks like it belongs to:

❏ a) you! Your cool collection of treasures matches your unique personality.

❏ b) a five-year-old. One more stuffed animal piled on your ruffled bedspread and the ASPCA is going to come set them free.

❏ c) Miss Typical Teen America—right down to the must-have posters on the wall.

2 Most of the furniture in your room:

❏ a) has a special story behind it or relates to some important memories.

❏ b) got passed down to you from someone else.

❏ c) just seemed to show up one day after one of your parents' decorating sprees.

3 You use your walls:

❏ a) like a gallery, carefully hanging things of artistic or sentimental value for all the world to see.

❏ b) like a scrapbook, with memories from the past.

❏ c) mostly just to hold up the ceiling.

4 The paint or wallpaper:

❏ a) goes with a look you really like.

❏ b) hasn't changed since your sister moved out.

❏ c) color-coordinates with the curtains and rug.

5 Walking into your room feels most like:

❏ a) entering a secret hideaway.

❏ b) entering a time warp.

❏ c) going to a hotel room, where nothing stands out.

6 As far as the fragrance in your room goes:

❏ a) you like to use potpourri, sachets, candles, or incense to create a pleasant atmosphere.

❏ b) even blindfolded you would recognize that mysterious smell it has always had.

❏ c) you could call it a fine blend of dirty gym clothes and stale Cheetos.

7 You have rearranged your stuff:

❑ a) several times since the school year started.

❑ b) on the rare occasions when you needed to make room for something new.

❑ c) once before, but nobody seemed to notice.

8 Everyone has stuffed animals. You have:

❑ a) a few that have major meaning to you.

❑ b) a collection that has multiplied every year since you were born.

❑ c) a few mingled in with all the other miscellaneous junk on your shelves.

9 When you get a little down in the dumps:

❑ a) it helps to be alone in your private space.

❑ b) your room makes you feel nostalgic.

❑ c) you just want to get out of your room and go somewhere else.

SCORING

Total the number of answers you checked for each letter. Then read the description that corresponds to the letter you checked most often—and find out what your bedroom says about you.

YOU'VE GOT THE LOOK   MOSTLY As

Your decorating style matches your personality perfectly, and according to Nancy Boothe, a Virginia decorator, nothing matters more than that in a bedroom. "I usually try to find out what the person likes before I do anything else." Just because you happen to sleep there, Boothe says, doesn't mean your bedroom has to look like one. She recommends incorporating your hobbies and talents as much as possible. Make your bedroom a "Wow!" room.

GET A MAKEOVER   MOSTLY Bs

Lava lamps and disco balls qualify as retro, but Raggedy Ann curtains and Winnie-the-Pooh nightlights scream, "Give your room a face-lift!" That doesn't mean you should toss those great old memories in the nearest dumpster, but try to blend the past with the present. Dividing the room into areas can help you accomplish that. And things that don't seem to fit—like that glow-in-the-dark Tigger—can be put away in a closet or attic for safekeeping.

TOO BLAND   MOSTLY Cs

A million things distinguish you from everyone else your age, but at the moment, your room isn't one of them. If you hired Boothe, she would hand you a stack of magazines and ask you to pick out some looks you love, then she would take it from there. But you don't need to hire a pro. Boothe has seen really impressive rooms that teens decorated on their own.

Just add some interesting touches. Hanging your ballet slippers or high tops in a cool place can speak volumes. As Boothe says, "The important thing is that your personality should come out in your room." Go on, get creative!

What's Your Guy Type?

Are you totally hot for a certain guy and desperately trying to grab his attention? Take this quiz to figure out if you know how to win him over.

The best way to get a guy who's compatible with you is to be yourself. If a boy doesn't dig you for you, you should set your sights on one who will. But if your type and his type match, you're golden.

WHAT'S HIS TYPE?

Check off the description below that comes closest to describing your drool-worthy guy du jour:

☐ Class Clown: This guy, whose hero is Kramer from *Seinfeld,* really knows how to pack a punch line. He probably does a killer impersonation of your homeroom teacher, too.

☐ All-American Jock: This guy is a real team player and almost never seen without a number on his chest. He's always in training for some sport—be it baseball, football, or hockey—and never late for practice.

☐ Everybody's Best Bud: This guy is a total sweetheart who knows everyone's name and has a zillion friends. He usually has a smile on his face and a compliment on the tip of his tongue to brighten your day.

☐ Shy Guy: He hangs with the same people day in, day out, and rarely speaks unless he has to. You'd find him in the back of the class with his head buried in the books—and probably blushing.

WHAT'S YOUR STYLE?

Now answer the following questions and see if there is serious chemistry between your crush and wonderful li'l you:

1 You go to the mall and see him hanging by the hot dog stand, and he's got a big glob of mustard dripping from his chin. Your best bet is to:

❑ a) go up and punch him on the arm, saying you hope his aim on the basketball court is better than his aim in the food court.

❑ b) put a glob of mustard on your chin and go tell him you heard mustard goatees were the new "in" thing.

❑ c) stand to the side and casually wipe your chin over and over till he gets the hint.

❑ d) hand him a stack of napkins with a smile and a wink.

2 You see him standing on the sidelines at your spring dance, and you decide to make your move. You:

❑ a) tell him dancing is a great calf workout, then ask if he'd like to join you for a little aerobic activity.

❑ b) challenge him to a dance contest—whoever does the goofiest dance step wins a package of Pez, to be delivered before first period Monday morning.

❑ c) ask him if these social situations make him feel as stupid as they make you feel, then ask him if he'd like to dance...that way, you can feel stupid together.

❏ d) give him a sisterly punch on the arm and tell him it's your turn to dance with the sweetest guy in the room.

3 Your best friend is throwing a birthday bash, and your guy said he'd be there. You wear:

❏ a) your beloved baseball cap.

❏ b) a Dr. Seuss baby T.

❏ c) an unusual necklace that he could comment on.

❏ d) your comfiest Levi's.

4 It's the last day of school, and your crush asks you to autograph his yearbook. You write:

❏ a) "This year you scored points for the school and with me."

❏ b) "Knock knock. Who's there? Orange. Orange who? Orange you going to miss me this summer?"

❏ c) "Even though you try not to be noticed, you didn't succeed with me."

❏ d) "Time may pass, but friends like you are forever."

5 The student council is selling Candy-Grams, and you decide to send the guy of your dreams one. The confection you choose is:

❏ a) a Power Bar.

❏ b) Pop Rocks.

❏ c) homemade cookies.

❏ d) Hershey's Kisses.

6 Your bro is having a few people over to watch *The X-Files,* and your guy is one of his invited guests. Your seduction move is to:

❏ a) wait for the commercial, then ask him if he wants to shoot some hoops.

❏ b) bust out a can of Silly String and slime the boys during a spooky, spine-tingling scene.

❏ c) sit near him and pass him some popcorn with a smile.

❏ d) treat him just like you treat your brother.

7 You see your crush sitting at a near-empty table in the caf. You:

❏ a) toss a chicken nugget his way and tell him to think fast.

❏ b) plop right down and tell him in your best mom voice that if he doesn't clean his plate, he'll be sent to bed without dessert.

❏ c) sit near him and make a comment about how gag-worthy the pizza burgers are today.

❏ d) sit down and ask if he's going to finish those celery sticks.

8 You're swimming a few laps when you spy your guy horsing around by the pool. You:

❏ a) challenge him to a game of Marco Polo.

❏ b) swim up behind him and hum the Jaws theme music.

❏ c) smile and ask if he comes here often.

❏ d) sneak up and pull him into the deep end.

9 Your friend dares you to pass a note to your crush. You:

❏ a) jot something down, fold the note like a football, then jet it across the room.

❏ b) strain your brain for your funniest one-liner, then pass it away.

❏ c) say no way! (Your guy would turn as red as a tomato if you went through with it.)

❏ d) write about whatever comes to mind, then hand it to him after class.

Scoring

Total the number of answers you checked for each letter. Then read the description below of the guy type that corresponds to the letter you checked most often.

Now read on for more info on the key to your guy's heart.

SPORT BOY SCORER   MOSTLY As

Getting the attention of a jock is *no problemo*. If you're at all athletic, appeal to his sporty side and treat him like one of the guys. While it's true that athletic boys *loooove* the thrill of the chase, be sure to slow down enough so he can catch you—or you might just be spinning your wheels.

CLOWN CATCHER   MOSTLY Bs

Class clowns definitely notice girls who are witty and dig laughing out loud. Sound like you? If you're a whiz at shooting him one-liners and flashing a funny face at the perfect moment, you could without a doubt tickle his funny bone. Just remember to be serious once in a while, or he might think that you consider him a joke, too.

SHY GUY STEALER   mostly Cs

You could definitely give that shy guy a reason to lift his head from the book he's buried in, as long as you can handle his quietness. If you're a pro at showing your interest without going overboard, you're good to go, 'cause it's a sure way to wow him without scaring him off. But be careful not to wait for him to make the first move . . . or you could be waiting forever.

CHUM CHARMER   mostly Ds

If earning a friend-boy's affection comes totally natural to you, you've chosen the right guy type. Treat him like a bro and play it cool as a cucumber, and your at-ease ways could definitely catch his attention. But be sure to indicate at some point that you want to be more than friends, or else he may consider you another bud to add to his collection.

What's Your Self-Image?

Do you see yourself through oh-so-realistic eyes or a fun-house mirror? Take this quiz to find out what you think of your looks and what your self-image means.

1 When people compliment you on how great you look, you:

❑ a) thank them.

❑ b) wonder what they're really trying to tell you. Do they mean you don't usually look good?

❑ c) argue with them. "Yeah, right—did you see this zit? And my hair's a total wreck."

2 If on a rare special occasion you and your friends go on an eatfest, consuming more fat and junk food than you usually allow yourself, afterward you:

❑ a) resolve to balance it out by watching your calories the next day and making sure to get a little extra exercise.

❑ b) stand in front of the mirror, worrying and feeling guilty, looking to see where the bulges have formed.

❑ c) get down-in-the-dumps depressed. Then it's marathon, no-pain, no-gain workout sessions and sweets deprivation for a week.

3 When you try on clothes in a store, you usually:

❏ a) find a few things you like without a problem.

❏ b) bring a friend along for a second opinion.

❏ c) try to sneak out to the mirrors when no one is watching, get frustrated with your reflection, curse the fluorescent lighting, and leave empty-handed.

4 When you hear your friends complaining about their minor imperfections, you:

❏ a) reassure them. Tell them that you have thin eyelashes too, and you also wish your parents had given you long-leg genes, but hey, it's not that big a deal! Then you remind them you're still the coolest bunch of girls around.

❏ b) tell them to change the subject! Their complaints just remind you of all your own flaws, which you would prefer to forget.

❏ c) feel comforted. You're thankful that your friends have as many problems with their looks as you do.

5 Your fashion strategy could best be described as:

❏ a) maximizing your resources. You bought that blue sweater to bring out your eyes and that belt to show off the results of all those crunches you've been doing. You know what your best features are, and you know how to work 'em!

❏ b) camouflage. The staples of your wardrobe include baggy pants, big skirts that touch the floor, and

T-shirts ten sizes too big. How can anyone find fault with your body if they can't even find it?

❏ c) repair. You're constantly identifying your worst appearance disasters and trying to fix them. A huge chunk of your allowance goes to coverup sticks and self-tanning gels, and you've considered asking for a nose job for your birthday.

6 At the beach, you spend most of your time:

❏ a) goofing off and having a blast! You walk, swim, play volleyball, and hang out with friends. Stressing out at the beach would be a sin!

❏ b) trying to get a tan without getting noticed. If anyone from school saw you in a bathing suit, the only color you'd get is a nice blush red.

❏ c) wishing evil curses on all the perfect-looking girls you see running around in thongs.

7 When the best-looking guy at the party is staring at you, it makes you:

❏ a) feel flattered and thrilled. You stare right back!

❏ b) nervous. Why is he staring at you? You could go talk to him, find out if he's dating anyone.... Nah, you figure that with all the other pretty girls around, he must be looking at someone standing behind you.

❏ c) anxious. Is there something in your teeth?

8 When your friends pull out their cameras, you:

❑ a) strike a pose! It's fun to have your picture taken.

❑ b) offer to take the pictures. That way you don't have to worry about being in any of the shots.

❑ c) suck in your stomach, fix your hair, and try to hide in the back of the crowd.

9 Your body priority is:

❑ a) strength. After all, strength of body, mind, and spirit is what beauty is all about!

❑ b) weight management. If you could just be a different weight, you'd be satisfied.

❑ c) perfection. You won't be satisfied with anything less.

Scoring

Give yourself one point for every A, two points for every B, and three points for every C.

PERFECTLY OBSESSED   27 TO 22 POINTS

The way you responded to these questions ought to help you realize that you spend way too much time putting yourself down. You can start feeling better about yourself by doing two things: First, take a close, admiring look at yourself. Forget about those self-criticisms for a minute and make a list of your most wonderful features. Grab that list whenever you feel doubts creep up. Remember, people stand out for their exceptional qualities, like those sparkling eyes of yours, not those minor imperfections that everyone has. Second, keep in mind that getting a good look at yourself takes more than a mirror. Donna DeGaetani, a Los Angeles psychotherapist, says a poor self-image could indicate you need to work on some deeper identity issues. "Accept that a good feeling about yourself does not come just from how you look," DeGaetani says. "Try to form a connection with an older female. Talk to someone who has gone through these feelings and can help give you some perspective." Believe it or not, lots of people struggle with low self-esteem. Even Cindy Crawford probably once felt the same way you do!

MISS MODESTY   21 TO 16 POINTS

Why are you hiding? Behind those baggy clothes and underneath those insecurities is a girl with her own unique and wonderful sense of style. That means you can stop trying to look like Kate Moss, Naomi Campbell, or anyone else for that matter, and take pride in your own (inner and outer) beauty. Try putting a big smile on your face the next time you find yourself in front of your mirror or your friend's camera. You're beautiful and you should be proud of it! Learning how to accept praise is an important step in feeling comfortable with yourself. DeGaetani says, "Practice accepting compliments by saying, 'Thank you,' and believe that the compliments are authentically given." Next time someone tells you that your haircut looks incredible, resist the urge to describe how ugly it looked when you rolled out of bed in the morning. There's nothing wrong with acknowledging your special qualities. When you put yourself down too often, you don't just convince other people of your real or imaginary faults, you convince yourself.

SITTING PRETTY   15 TO 9 POINTS

Don't be surprised if all your friends say how much they envy you. They should! You have what every girl wants—and deserves—but few know how to find: a strong sense of your own beauty and self-worth. As DeGaetani puts it, "All of our attractiveness does not have to come from appearance. A person is beautiful if she projects a sense of inner strength, a sense of connectedness to the world, and a desire to participate in life." Just by feeling confident, you make it easy for other people to believe in you too. Everyone has occasional doubts about her appearance, but you know the trick is to look past those doubts so you can accept and love yourself for who you are. If you could bottle your confidence, you'd make a fortune!

Are You Right- or Left-Brained?

That big gray muscle in your head does more than just store information. The "strong" side of your brain can determine what you like, how you view things, and what you're good at doing. According to Doug Davis, Ph.D., professor of psychology at Haverford College, in Pennsylvania, figuring out which side of your brain is dominant can help you identify your strong and weak points. For example, right-brained people groove on creative freethinking, while planning and analyzing suit the left-brained just fine.

Check off the statements that most apply to you to find out if you're a lefty or righty.

1. When I pick up a new CD, I read the notes about the band inside.

2. When I pick up a new CD, I look at the cover design.

3. I'd rather figure out a math problem than write a poem.

4. I'd rather paint a picture than complete a science experiment.

5. If I fight with a friend, I write about it in my diary to figure it out.

6. If I fight with a friend, I do something that makes me feel better—like eat chocolate.

7. My room is usually neat.

- [ ] 8. My room is usually a disaster area.

- [ ] 9. I like playing team sports, like basketball, volleyball, and baseball.

- [ ] 10. I dig solo sports, like running, hiking, or biking.

- [ ] 11. When I write a paper, I outline what I want to write, then start writing.

- [ ] 12. When I write a paper, I just start writing and see what happens.

- [ ] 13. I wear whatever is in style and follow clothes trends.

- [ ] 14. I wear whatever I feel like wearing at the time.

- [ ] 15. I listen to cool, new bands and whatever is on the popular radio station.

- [ ] 16. I listen to older music or whatever I'm in the mood for.

- [ ] 17. When I meet new people, I remember their names.

- [ ] 18. When I meet new people, I remember what they're wearing.

- [ ] 19. I like being organized and planning ahead.

- [ ] 20. I like going with the flow and doing whatever seems like fun.

- [ ] 21. I'm usually on time.

- [ ] 22. I'm usually late.

☐ 23. I make my bed almost every day.

☐ 24. I make my bed when I feel like it.

☐ 25. When I listen to music I like, I sing along because I know the words.

☐ 26. When I listen to music I like, I move with the beat.

☐ 27. I usually organize parties or the things I do with my friends.

☐ 28. I usually go along with whatever someone has already planned.

☐ 29. If I had a diary, I'd write in it every night.

☐ 30. If I had a diary, I'd write in it when I felt like writing in it.

☐ 31. I remember all of my friends' birthdays.

☐ 32. I remember all of my friends' favorite colors.

☐ 33. When I watch TV, I find out what's on, then decide what to watch.

☐ 34. When I watch TV, I channel surf until I find something I like.

☐ 35. My class notebooks are color coded and neat.

☐ 36. My class notebooks are part doodle pad, part barely readable notes.

☐ 37. My clothes are mostly solid colors or outfits that are one print.

☐ 38. My clothes are a mixture of colors, prints, and styles.

☐ 39. I eat healthy food because it's good for me.

☐ 40. I eat some healthy food, some junk food—it just depends on my mood.

☐ 41. When I exercise, I usually have a set routine that I follow.

☐ 42. When I exercise, I usually work on whatever part feels flabby.

☐ 43. If I had a bad hair day, I'd wear a hat or pony-tail.

☐ 44. If I had a bad hair day, I'd point it out to my friends.

☐ 45. My friends think I'm a little neurotic.

☐ 46. My friends think I'm a little scatterbrained.

Scoring

If you checked mostly odd-numbered statements (1, 3, 5, etc.), you're a left-brainer. This means you're a thinker, a planner, and a talker. You know how to analyze situations and make clear decisions based on what you think. "People seek you out for advice because you have a level head," Davis says. "Teachers love you because you remember answers and are good at memorizing."

The downside of being strictly left-brained is being a little too regimented. You might be a bit too structured for some people, and that can get you into trouble. "Left-brainers tend to talk too much because they spend so much time trying to explain themselves," Davis says. "They're too caught up in the tiny details of something to see the whole picture."

If you checked mostly even-numbered statements (2, 4, 6, etc.), you're a right-brainer. Being a righty means being creative, spontaneous, and perhaps even scatterbrained. You're a feeler, so most of what you do and think is based on how it makes you feel. "Right-brainers are impulsive and easygoing," says Davis. "They're very visually oriented, which means they see the big picture before they see the little things that make up the picture."

The problem with right-brainers always "feeling" and "doing" is that they may not do enough thinking. "There are rules you're supposed to be following, and sometimes right-brainers forget that," says Davis. "They're easily distracted and can have a hard time focusing on jobs that require planning or organization."

If you're an even mix of the two sides, don't worry. Most people are a little of both. "The goal is to use both halves of your brain. The most creative and successful people are a good combination of the two," Davis says. And remember, Socrates said that knowing yourself lets you capitalize on your strengths and minimize your weaknesses.

FLEXING YOUR GRAY MATTER

Just like any other muscle, if you let one side of your brain take over, the other side withers. So how do you pump up your weak side? Try these cerebral crunches to keep your whole brain fit.

RIGHT-BRAINERS

Wear a watch and make a conscious effort to be on time.

Make a Things to Do list every day.

Set aside time for certain tasks, like homework and household chores.

Memorize all your friends' phone numbers.

Create outlines or plans for tackling papers and homework problems.

Alphabetize your movie collection, books, or stack of CDs.

Read bus schedules or make a mental note of store hours.

Take ten deep breaths next time you feel impulsive about doing something. If the impulse is still there, do it. If not, don't.

LEFT-BRAINERS

Look at pictures and make up stories about the people in them.

Make someone else plan the next party or get-together.

Paint something without sketching it first.

Throw away your Things to Do list one day a week and do what you feel like doing.

Wear funky socks.

Take a blank sheet of paper and write or draw whatever comes to mind first—words, pictures, or phrases.

Shake up your morning routine—go for a walk or sleep really late.

Make up new words and use them in conversation. Don't explain what they mean unless someone asks.

How Easily Do You Make Friends?

Are you quick to bond with new buds, or is making friends totally traumatic? Test your social skills with this quiz.

1 The track team is traveling to an out-of-town meet. You've got your sleeping arrangements all worked out with your running mates, when you notice one girl has no one to bunk with. Without any hesitation, you offer to share your room with her.

❏ Yeah, that's me.　　　❏ No, not me.

2 The new girl at school wears the funkiest footwear you've ever seen. Since you have a major shoe fetish, you invite her to go shopping this weekend.

❏ Yeah, that's me.　　　❏ No, not me.

3 Mom is convinced that you and her college roommate's daughter would get along like two peas in a pod. Mom's even promised you'll call her. You decide not to hold your mom's matchmaking against the girl and give her a ring.

❏ Yeah, that's me.　　　❏ No, not me.

4 The drama club didn't recognize you as the diva you are and gave the lead in *Romeo and Juliet* to someone else. You were offered the role of a lowly servant. Ouch! But you decide being involved is still more fun than going home alone.

❏ Yeah, that's me.   ❏ No, not me.

5 You're at Grandma's for the holidays and notice a girl next door who looks about your age. You decide to introduce yourself—it's either that or watch the cooking channel with Granny.

❏ Yeah, that's me.   ❏ No, not me.

6 You've just started at a new school and don't really know anyone yet. You overhear a group of girls in math class making plans to catch the new Leo flick and seize the opportunity to ask if you can tag along.

❏ Yeah, that's me.   ❏ No, not me.

7 It's Friday night, your friends are away, and you're bored out of your mind. A friend from summer camp calls and invites you to a party. You won't know anyone, but she promises to introduce you to lots of cute guys. "I'll be right there," you tell her.

❏ Yeah, that's me.   ❏ No, not me.

8 None of your buds want to go on the class camping trip, but you can't wait to pitch your tent and roast those s'mores. You sign up and hope

you don't get stuck with someone who snores.

❑ Yeah, that's me.   ❑ No, not me.

9 Your best bud is spending more and more time hanging out with some girls who don't go to your school. You're worried she's drifting away, so you suggest a slumber party that includes the new girls. This way, all of you can get to know each other.

❑ Yeah, that's me.   ❑ No, not me.

10 At your friend's birthday party, you meet a really nice girl who shares your obsession with Andrew Keegan. As you're leaving, she says, "Let's get together sometime." You don't hear from her for a while, so you decide to take the initiative and give her a ring.

❑ Yeah, that's me.   ❑ No, not me.

Scoring

Give yourself two points for every "Yeah" answer, one point for every "No." Then add up your total score.

AS EASY AS 1-2-3   17 TO 20 POINTS

There's an old Irish saying that goes something like this: "There are no strangers here. Only friends you haven't met yet." You can walk into a crowded room and, within minutes, joke with strangers like you've known each other forever. Squeezing new friends into your busy social calendar can take up a lot of energy, so don't spread yourself too thin. Even with a packed social life, you could find yourself alone on a Friday night. Casual acquaintances won't wait for your call like best friends will.

FAIRLY FRIENDLY   14 TO 16 POINTS

You're definitely no wallflower. You've got great buds, but sometimes you find it tricky making new friends. Carol Weston, author of *Girltalk: All the Stuff Your Sister Never Told You,* has some helpful tips: Be a good listener since people love to talk about themselves; develop charm because making people feel wonderful means they'll probably feel the same about you; don't dump on strangers since no one's into a whiner. Mostly, be the kind of person you'd like to know.

HOME ALONE   10 TO 13 POINTS

Are you painfully shy or sorta antisocial? Maybe it's a bit of both. You'd rather sit alone than invite the new girl to hang out after school. "You can get by without being popular; you can live without a boyfriend; you can survive without one particular best friend. But if you have no friends, you're missing out," says Weston. It might be tough overcoming your shyness, but consider the lonely alternative. So arm yourself with a smile, and you'll probably find others smiling right back at you.

How Open-Minded Are You?

Do you let stereotypes junk up your brain waves and rule your decisions? Read on and find out.

1 Your best bud walks into first period, and—whoa!—her brown hair is now bright blue. You:

❑ a) pretend you've never seen her before in your life.

❑ b) feel a little embarrassed but talk to her anyway.

❑ c) are sorta surprised, but hey, she's still the same person.

2 A guy in the computer club asks you out. You:

❑ a) say no way. Everybody knows cyberboys are nerds.

❑ b) give him a chance, even though he's not your usual type.

❑ c) are totally psyched for the chance to surf the Net with a supreme tour guide like him.

3 A girl who's your total opposite is assigned to be your lab partner. You:

❑ a) tell the teacher you're allergic to the chick's perfume, then you switch partners with someone else.

❏ b) think it'll be a big drag, but you tolerate her to salvage your grade.

❏ c) are thrilled by the opportunity to bond with someone so different.

4 You just won tickets on the radio to a hip-hop concert, but you're more into alternative tunes. You:

❏ a) decide to blow it off. It won't be any fun, so why bother?

❏ b) go anyway to check out the scene, but bail before the band goes on.

❏ c) put on some baggy pants and dive into the hip-hop thing for a night.

5 Your cousin—who has great taste—goes on a shopping spree and buys you a wild outfit, the kind you'd never wear. You:

❏ a) tell her it's not for you.

❏ b) accept it graciously, hang it in the back of your closet, and take it out only on Halloween.

❏ c) wear it out that night. Hey, if she pictured it on you, it probably looks rad.

6 Your dad announces he's taking the whole family on a trip, and you're way psyched—that is, until you find out the destination is a tiny town in the middle of nowhere. You:

❏ a) tell him it'll be a total bore and ask to stay with your best bud that week instead.

❏ b) go, but stay in the cabin and bury your head in *Sweet Valley High* books all week.

❏ c) can't wait. You're determined to meet as many of the locals as you possibly can.

7 There's a new foreign-exchange student in your fifth-period class. You:

❏ a) give him the cold shoulder—hey, you probably don't even speak the same language.

❏ b) smile his way, but don't bother with conversation.

❏ c) introduce yourself, then ask him to join you and your friends at the game Friday night.

8 You're at the movies with your best bud. You have your heart set on the latest Leonardo DiCaprio drool-fest, but she wants to see a foreign flick. You:

❏ a) tell her if you wanted to read, you would have gone to the library. After all, subtitles are a pain.

❏ b) compromise—if she'll watch Leo tonight, you'll watch the foreign flick tomorrow.

❏ c) say you're up for a cinematic adventure, then imagine you're in another country as you follow her into the theater.

9 Your crush wants you to go bungee jumping with him. He sees you hesitate and asks if you're scared. You say:

❏ a) "Only crazy people risk their lives for something as stupid as jumping."

❏ b) "A little—let me start with something smaller and work my way up to this."

❏ c) "Who wouldn't be? I'm into facing my fears, but let me clear it with my parents first."

10 The most popular girl in school moves in next door. You:

❏ a) figure she'll be a total snob and make sure you snub her before she snubs you.

❏ b) wave at her and see if she returns the gesture.

❏ c) bring over a batch of brownies and say you're psyched someone cool moved in.

Scoring

Total the number of answers you checked for each letter. Then read the description that corresponds to the letter you checked most often to find out how open-minded you are.

SORRY, WE'RE CLOSED   MOSTLY As

Even though you may not realize it, your mind is more closed than Pizza Hut at 4 A.M. You often judge people before getting to know them and hesitate before trying anything new. "Someone who is close-minded relies heavily on her preconceived notions," warns Kathleen Hoover, a New York–based psychotherapist. "She thinks she's not going to like something or someone, and the buck stops there." Try giving things a chance before turning your nose up at them. Who knows—you might be pleasantly surprised!

HALFWAY OPEN, HALFWAY SHUT

You have your open-minded moments, when you feel like you could do anything or befriend anybody, but most of the time your old stereotypes get in the way. "You're curious about new things and new people, but you're stopped by the part of yourself that isn't so adventurous," explains Hoover. "Your stereotypes stop you from embracing life to the fullest." So the next time your close-minded self pipes up, tell her to shut up—then follow your heart.

OPEN 24 HOURS

Your mind is totally open. You're into new experiences and don't buy into stereotypes of any sort. "If you're this open-minded, you probably don't judge others on the basis of appearance or reputation," says Hoover. "You give new people and new opportunities a chance." Since you're so open, you often dive into any new experience that presents itself. Just remember to use common sense—saying no in a dangerous situation doesn't mean you're close-minded. It means you're careful, and there's nothing wrong with that.

What's the Best Career for You?

Someday in the not-so-distant future, your school days are gonna be over. But then what? When it's time to take on the "real world," will you do it in a business suit or a lab coat? Set your mind to it, and you can do just about anything. To see in what direction your talents and interests could lead you, take this quiz.

Part I: Skills

Put a check next to each statement that applies to you.

_____ ■ I tend to do better in classes like math, science, and economics.

_____ ❤ When it comes to extracurricular activities, I prefer the debate team to the school newspaper.

_____ ● My best courses are usually English or journalism.

_____ ■ I find it pretty easy to keep to a budget and manage to save some of the money I earn for expensive stuff.

_____ ❤ If a teacher let me choose between an oral or written report, I'd pick the oral report.

_____ ● I have at least one hobby that involves working with my hands (drawing, pottery, baking, etc.).

_____ ■ I get a kick out of taking things apart—like dolls, clocks, or toys—even if I may not be able to get them back together!

____ ❤ When I hop on the Internet, I go straight for the chat rooms.

____ ● I love telling stories to my friends and can often make events sound better than they actually were.

____ ■ If people ask me for directions, I either draw them a map or give them approximate distances and street names to get them where they need to be.

____ ● If people ask me for directions, I tend to give them landmarks and descriptions of the area instead of street names.

____ ❤ At the moment, most of my friends know which guy I have a crush on.

____ ■ When a friend has a problem, I help her by analyzing the situation and offering suggestions.

____ ❤ When a friend has a problem, I help her by offering sympathy and a shoulder to cry on.

____ ● The idea of spending a rainy Saturday tucked away in my room with a few good books sounds absolutely great.

____ ■ If I go out to a restaurant with a group of friends, I'm usually the one who ends up figuring out what everyone owes on the bill.

____ ❤ When I go to a party, there's rarely a dull moment for me. I dance and chat the whole night through.

____ ● I tend to have really vivid and sometimes off-the-wall dreams.

____ ■ If I were to break my in-line skates, I'd try hard to fix them before I'd even think of taking them to a repair shop.

_____ ♥ If my friends and I were planning a night out and there was something I really wanted to do, I'd be able to convince my friends to do it.

_____ ● I take signing yearbooks seriously. I write something personal, thoughtful, or humorous to friends instead of the standard, "Have a great summer—I'll miss you."

_____ ■ Even when it's not required, I always make an outline before I write a paper.

_____ ● I go nutso if I have to sit in class for too long— it totally stifles my creativity.

_____ ♥ If a teacher separates the class into discussion groups, I'm most often the person in my group to get the discussion going.

_____ ● I prefer games like charades to games like chess.

_____ ■ I love mind games and brain teasers.

_____ ♥ I love to be the center of attention.

Part II: Interests

Rate your top three school subjects. (1=most fave, 2=second-most fave, 3=third-most fave)

_____ Art. . . . . CR

_____ Auto shop . . . . SE, SC

_____ Business class . . . . BS, DY, ME

_____ Computers . . . . BS, SC

_____ Economics . . . . BS

_____ English/writing . . . . CR, BS, ME

_____ Foreign language . . . . DY, ME

____ Government/political science....... DY, HE, ME

____ Health .... MD, HE

____ History .... BS, HE

____ Home economics.................... HE, SE

____ Math (algebra,calculus, etc.)........... MD, SC

____ Metal shop........................ SC, SE

____ Music .... CR

____ Physical education .... SE, HE, CR

____ Psychology/sociology .... DY, HE, MD

____ Science (biology, physics, etc.)......... MD, SC

____ Typing .... BS, HE, SC, ME

____ Wood shop .... CR, SE

PART III: PUTTING IT ALL TOGETHER

Reviewing Part I, count the number of statements you checked for each shape, then write the totals below:

■:____   ♥:____   ●:____

Each of these areas represents a skills group. Finding out where your skills lie can help show you which fields may come more easily or naturally for you. In each of the three groups, there are a ton of specific job categories. Part II will help you identify your interests and pick a more specific job category.

■ LOGIC AND DATA GROUP

Your skills lie in areas that involve numbers, machines, and objects. You like order and tend to come up with answers based on logic rather than emotions.

♥ People Group

You are best suited for working with people, whether by motivating them or by helping them. Your ideal work environment involves constant interaction with others.

● Creative Group

Your best talents lie in your creativity, either with written or spoken words, or with images. You need a work environment that enables you to use your creativity; you're likely to get antsy in a nine-to-five workplace that keeps you chained to a desk.

Now, moving on to Part II, write in the two-letter codes that appear alongside your favorite subjects. If any two-letter code appears more than once, it's the area you're most strongly suited for.

1._____

2._____

3._____

Check out the following pages for specifics on what the codes mean. Look at the jobs listed under each skills category (logic and data; people; and creative). Those you are best suited for are the ones in both your skills group and your interests group. But take a close look at all of the job listings in your skills group; you may find that jobs from other interests groups appeal to you more. Circle the jobs or categories that you find interesting.

SKILLS CATEGORY: LOGIC AND DATA

INTEREST CATEGORIES:

BS: BUSINESS

Administrator	Lawyer
Advertising media planner	Manager
Bank teller	Salesperson
Banker	School administrator
Economist	Stockbroker
Hotel manager	

MD: MEDICINE

Dentist	Physical therapist
Dietitian/nutritionist	Surgeon
Doctor	Veterinarian
Nurse	X-ray technician
Ophthalmologist/optometrist	

SC: SCIENCE

Architect	Engineer
Biologist	Lab technician
Chemist	Mathematician
Computer programmer	Physicist

SKILLS CATEGORY: PEOPLE

INTEREST CATEGORIES:

DY: DYNAMIC/MOTIVATING

Advertising sales	Public relations/publicity
Entrepreneur	Producer
International business	Real estate agent
Lobbyist	Salesperson
Manager	Travel agent
Politician	

HE: HELPING/COUNSELING

Conservationist	Psychiatrist
Counselor	Psychologist
Librarian	Social worker
Minister	Teacher

SE: SERVICE

Day care center worker/owner	Medical assistant
Firefighter	Police officer
Flight attendant	Secretary
Homemaker	

SKILLS CATEGORY: CREATIVE

INTEREST CATEGORIES:

CR: CREATIVE

Actress	Model
Artist	Musician
Chef	Photographer
Fashion designer	Singer
Interior designer	Writer

ME: MEDIA

Broadcast journalist	Photojournalist
Director	Producer
Journalist	Radio broadcaster
Magazine editor	Reporter

PART IV: NOW WHAT?

Now that you've discovered a few of the careers you're currently suited for, it's up to you to take a further look at the individual job types to see if you're interested in pursuing any of them. Take your list of jobs to your school's guidance or career center to check them out. If your school doesn't have a guidance or career center, go to the library. There are many books out there to give you the nitty-gritty on just about every job you can imagine. Try:

• *Encyclopedia of Careers and Vocational Guidance.* William E. Hopke, ed. Maryland: Garret Park Press, updated regularly.

• *Occupational Outlook Handbook.* Bureau of Labor

Statistics. U.S. Government Printing Office, Washington, D.C.

- *What Color Is Your Parachute?* Richard N. Bolles. Berkeley: Ten Speed Press, updated annually.

- *Making a Living While Making a Difference.* Melissa Everett. New York: Bantam Books, 1995.

Are You an Optimist or a Pessimist?

Do you think life's just a big bowl of cherries—minus the pits? Or is the whole world out to get you?

1 You're at a party, and the boy of your dreams comes up and compliments you on your new GirlStar skirt. You think:

❏ a) It's true love. What he really meant to say is that he's head-over-heels for you.

❏ b) This could be the start of something. Maybe you ought to get to know each other a little better.

❏ c) He doesn't really mean it. He's probably just saying that because he feels sorry for you.

2 After spending an hour getting ready for the big dance, when you look in the mirror your reaction is:

❏ a) complete adoration. You are the cutest thing that you—and everyone else—ever saw.

❏ b) complete satisfaction. You've tried to make the most of your looks, and you know that your self-confidence shines through.

❏ c) complete disgust. You wish your straight hair was curly, your brown eyes were blue, and you'll be lucky if a boy even coughs in your direction.

3 You auditioned for the lead role in the school musical. The drama teacher says she'll announce who gets the part on Tuesday. When you haven't heard anything by Wednesday, you know:

❏ a) she's just saving the best for last. You sing better than Mariah, and at any moment you'll hear that you've won the lead.

❏ b) you did your best; it's just taking longer because there's a talented group of people to pick from.

❏ c) you blew it. You never should have tried in the first place. Everybody was probably laughing at you behind your back.

4 Your teacher has announced that there will be a creative-writing contest for your English class, and writing is your favorite subject. You:

❏ a) get busy planning what you'll do with the award. The teacher can't help but be impressed with your flair for fiction.

❏ b) pick the piece of writing that you feel best represents your style and hope for the best.

❏ c) don't even bother submitting anything. There's no way you'll win. It's best to just keep your work to yourself.

5 Your horoscope says a Taurus man will make the best boyfriend for you. It just so happens your crush is a Taurus. What do you think about that?

❏ a) You'll start pursuing him as soon as you put the horoscope down. How can he resist? It's in the stars.

❑ b) It would be nice if it were true. But it's best to spend some time with him, and see if the two of you could at least fall in like.

❑ c) Those things are never true. They're just a way to get your hopes raised, and that's something you never like to do.

6 It's summertime, and you've decided to get a job so you can treat yourself to one of those cute little hot-weather halter dresses. But you're really nervous about the whole interviewing thing. After your first interview, you leave feeling:

❑ a) like you aced it. You wouldn't be surprised if they offered you more money just to have you work for them.

❑ b) like you did okay, and maybe they'll call. You figure the more interviews you have, the more relaxed you'll be.

❑ c) like you blew it. You're sure they could tell your hands were shaking, and who needs a stupid halter dress anyway?

7 The most popular girl in school says hi to you in the hall—for the first time! But what did she really mean?

❑ a) "She wants to be my friend. She knows the girls she's been hanging out with don't have as great a personality as I do."

❑ b) "She wants to be friendly. Maybe I should ask her if she wants to hang out during lunch."

❏ c) "There's no way she'd ever want to be my friend.
She was probably saying hi as a dare."

8 You and your best bud have talked for weeks
about seeing the new Will Smith movie. You make
a date for an 8 P.M. showing, but at 7:55, she's a
no-show. You think:

❏ a) There are five minutes left. There's no way she'd
miss this movie. You'll wait outside until 8:30, just
to be sure.

❏ b) Maybe you should call her house and check to
make sure she's left. You hope nothing has gone
wrong.

❏ c) You ought to just go in and find a seat. She won't
show, and now you're mad 'cause you hate going to
movies by yourself.

9 Your best bud hasn't returned your call in three
days. At school, it seems like she's avoiding you.
You:

❏ a) think that she's probably just too busy to talk, and
she'll call when she gets a chance.

❏ b) hope that she's okay and write her a note
expressing your concern.

❏ c) frantically try to figure out what you did wrong.
You're sure you've done something to make her mad
at you.

10 Your friends have decided to have a birthday
party for one of the gang at the ice-skating
rink. But you've never skated in your life. You:

❏ a) run out and buy a cute skating outfit. When you hit the ice, your natural grace will make you look better than Tara Lipinski.

❏ b) hope that you'll do okay and ask one of your friends if she'll show you how to skate.

❏ c) lie and tell your buds you've got to go out of town that weekend. You wouldn't be caught dead falling on the ice. Somebody might laugh at you.

Scoring

Give yourself one point for every A, two points for every B, and three points for every C.

Perky Polly   10 to 17 points

You're so darn upbeat, you make Donna on *90210* look like a grouch. Although in the long run, it's better to be cheerful than down, the reality is that you're not always dealing with reality. If a situation is great and you see it as great, then everything's okay. But if a situation is bad, and you see it through rose-colored glasses, you have the potential to do yourself some harm. According to Suzanne Lopez, a family therapist practicing in Los Angeles, "You limit your real options. That could be to protect yourself from feeling the pain of disappointment." And disappointment is a natural part of life. Try seeing situations for what they are; you'll get to know yourself better in the process.

Sensible Sue   18 to 23 points

Welcome to reality! You know that life is a mixed bag of highs and lows. What's more, you trust yourself to ride the tide and make the best decisions for you. You're good at judging a situation without feeling too tied to the outcome. Says Lopez, "You can have a wish or a hope that something will turn out the way you want it." But as we all know, life doesn't always work out the way we hope it will. "But that disappointment won't devastate you," explains Lopez. "Something else valuable will happen in its place."

BLACK-CLOUD BELLE   24 TO 30 POINTS

Girlfriend, if you get any lower, you could play handball with the curb. Your negativity is keeping you from finding happiness, much less a fun time. "When you're negative all the time," says Lopez, "you're full of fear. It's a negative reflection of yourself." Your fears keep you from joining in the game of life. And ultimately you're setting yourself up for health problems, because we all know that less stress equals a healthier life. Take heart . . . you can change. According to Lopez, "Life is a process, and learning has a curve. When you try anything new, you may look foolish. But without trying, you keep yourself from being a person whom people can support and help."

Are You Impulsive?

Ever find yourself in a fix and wonder how the heck you got there? Think it's more fun to leap before you look?

1 On the way home from school, your best bud invites you to her house to watch Ricki Lake. But the rumor is that the teacher's gonna give a pop math quiz in class tomorrow. You:

❏ a) tell your friend you'll be right over. You just can't miss today's Ricki on punk rock girls and their nerd boyfriends. Besides, the quiz might not even happen. A rumor is just a rumor.

❏ b) tell her you have to study but you'll be over in time for *Dawson's Creek*.

❏ c) go home and study math for the rest of the night. Being prepared is number one in your book, and you want to make sure there's no way you'll get anything wrong.

2 Your father sent you to the store to buy some veggies for tonight's dinner, and when you get past the checkout line, you realize you've got some spare cash left over. Next door, the beauty supply store has that shade of Urban Decay polish you've been dying to try. You:

❏ a) make a beeline for the beauty supply store.

❏ b) call your dad from the store and ask if it's okay for you to spend the change on yourself. You tell him he can take it out of your allowance.

❑ c) put the change in your sock for safekeeping until you get home. You'll wait till you get your allowance and hope that the nail polish is still there by the time you've got the cash.

3 You're at the school dance wondering where your crush is. Suddenly, he shows up and tells you that he and the gang are going to the local pizza hangout. You know your mom is picking you up in an hour outside the school auditorium. You tell your crush:

❑ a) that leaving sounds great. You decide to tag along and figure Mom won't be ticked if you only keep her waiting a few extra minutes.

❑ b) to wait for you. You just have to call home and clear it with the 'rents.

❑ c) the invite sounds fun, but you promised your parents they could pick you up at the dance. Maybe he'd like to get together another time.

4 It's a beautiful day, and you're sitting in class with a teacher whose lecture on Columbus is sending you to lullabyland. You glance out the window and see your two best buds motioning for you to sneak out. You:

❑ a) raise your hand. When the teacher calls on you, you act like you're gonna toss your cookies. After you're excused, you bypass the nurse's office and make for the great outdoors and your pals.

❑ b) write a note telling your friends that you'll meet

them when school's out. When the teacher is writing on the blackboard, you send the note sailing through the window.

❏ c) ignore your friends. They shouldn't be distracting you from the discovery of America. You might learn something you could use when you're older.

5 You're walking through the mall with Mom when you pass Lady Foot Locker, and there in the window are the latest aerodynamic, ultralight, high-heeled sneakers—and they're hot pink, too. You think they're majorly ugly, but you notice the most popular girl in school standing in line to buy a pair. You:

❏ a) fall to your knees and beg Mom to buy you a pair. You tell her your popularity is on the line, and if she buys them, you'll wash the dishes for a month.

❏ b) decide to go home and sleep on it. The shoes aren't going anywhere, and if they're as ugly as you think they are, the most popular girl in school isn't gonna be number one for much longer when she wears those things.

❏ c) don't give them a second glance. You never buy the latest trend and instead prefer to wear classics in basic colors—that way you never go out of style, and you always match.

6 Your best friend is spending the night at your house, and your parents have gone out to dinner and a movie. You swore you wouldn't leave the house till they got home, but you can hear a raging party at your neighbor's house. You:

❏ a) sneak out of the house one at a time. With one of you keeping guard in case the 'rents show up early, there's no way you'll get busted.

❏ b) check out the party by hanging out on the back porch—that way, you're not technically leaving the house.

❏ c) decide to watch a movie on TV, even though you're a little tempted to grab a glimpse of the gala next door.

7 On your way to your Tuesday-night piano lesson, you pass the hottest guy in school shooting hoops in the park. He sees you and hollers for you to come talk to him. You tell him:

❏ a) "okay" and hang around until he asks you out, even though it means blowing off your piano lesson.

❏ b) "okay" but that you can only stop for a second. You've got an appointment you can't be late for.

❏ c) "no way" and ignore his attempts at getting your attention. Tori Amos didn't get famous by talking to boys.

8 You're standing in line at the school cafeteria when you spy a sinfully rich chocolate cake for dessert instead of the usual piece of fruit. Even though you've been on a health kick lately, you're so tempted that you:

❏ a) find you're staring at an empty plate. (You inhaled the cake before you even got to the cashier.)

❏ b) tell yourself you'll go to the health food store

after school for a vitamin-packed carob bar. It isn't chocolate, but it's close.

❏ c) put your tray back and leave the cafeteria. If you eat that piece of cake, who knows what you'll be tempted by next?

9 It's the weekend, and your mom has you slavin' away in the garage, clearing out the family's old junk. Your friends come by to say that they're going swimming at the local pool. You decide to:

❏ a) join them. You have to keep up your tan, and you can always clean the garage later.

❏ b) ask your mom if it's okay for you to clean for an hour, then join your friends. You tell her you'll finish the garage when you get home.

❏ c) keep working in the garage. Once you get started on something, you can't stop until it's done. Besides, running from the garage to the trash and back is all the aerobic exercise you need.

10 You're watching the latest *90210* and notice that Kelly has painted her bedroom dark purple. You think Kelly is way cool:

❏ a) and run right out to the hardware store for the darkest purple paint you can find. If it's good enough for Kelly, it's good enough for you.

❏ b) but think a shade of pale lavender might suit your room better. You decide to ask the 'rents first.

❏ c) but decide your good old white walls are just fine. Purple is a little too wild for you.

SCORING

Give yourself three points for every A, two points for every B, and one point for every C.

WILD CHILD   20 TO 24 POINTS

Party, party, party. You love an adventure and thrive on fun. Although it's normal to want fun and excitement, when you make decisions based only on what you want at that moment, you're not always doing what's best for you.

According to Susan Maxwell, a family therapist in Los Angeles, you may be trying to fit in with your friends instead. Look at the last five decisions you made. "Ask yourself, 'Am I comfortable with the decisions I made? Are my opinions, values, and beliefs as important as my friends'?'" says Maxwell. Just stop and think. "Figure out who you are and what you want, and get the courage to be that person."

CHICK IN CHARGE   14 TO 19 POINTS

You're secure enough in yourself to go your own way, rather than following the crowd. "Even though you want to be liked by your friends," says Maxwell, "you don't lose sight of what you want and what's important to you." You're more goal oriented, and you've figured out that the best way to have good relationships with your friends is by just being yourself. You act on what's best for you instead of trying to please your friends, and they respect you for it.

SAFETY FIRST   8 TO 13 POINTS

Time to loosen up. Have some fun. Although it's great to be responsible, it's also important to be a little spontaneous. "If you have an automatic response of no to everything," explains

Maxwell, "you're not really asserting your needs." You may be scared to take a risk, or perhaps you don't feel like you fit in with your friends. You can change if you want to. If you're accomplishing your goals, that's terrific. But make sure you take time to figure out what you really feel about situations before you automatically dismiss them. You'll be a happier, calmer person—and you might even have more fun, too.

Can You Trust Your Friends?

Choosing the right friends is an art. It takes a little chemistry, a lot of trust, and a bit of intuition.

1 Your friend just got busted for passing notes in class and has to stay after school for detention— again! When she tells the story the next day, she:

❏ a) whines endlessly about her evil teacher and how unfair he was to torture her with an entire hour of total boredom.

❏ b) invents an amazingly racy story about how she got into trouble, so everyone'll think she's wild.

❏ c) tells the true story quickly. Who wants to relive the nightmare of detention?

2 You and your buds pride yourselves on being a tight circle, so when new people who don't usually hang with you wander near:

❏ a) they just keep on walking. Everyone knows your group is way exclusive.

❏ b) your friends either make fun of them or make them feel like they don't belong. Who needs new friends when you've got each other?

❏ c) they get sucked into the fun and excitement your group thrives on.

3 One of your teachers pulls you aside after class and encourages you to submit your latest short story to the school's literary magazine. You're so psyched! When you bolt to tell your friends, they:

❏ a) tease that you might be turning into an ultrageek.

❏ b) congratulate you but immediately go back to talking about next weekend's big bash.

❏ c) support you all the way. They always knew you were a rising star.

4 Your parents have been fighting all month, and it's starting to get you down. When a friend asks you what the deal is with your attitude, you:

❏ a) clam up and claim that everything's great. Why bring someone else down with you?

❏ b) confide in her all the way. You can always trust her not to tell, and the same goes for her when she needs to confide in you.

❏ c) mumble something about PMS and make a quick exit. Last time you told your friend about your problems, everyone at school found out too!

5 After a Monday that started with a killer test and ended with the boy of your dreams flirting with an icky girl, all you want to do is go home and hide under the covers—which would mean canceling your usual Monday-night pizza plans with your buds. You:

❏ a) drag yourself to the pizza place. Your friends'll talk about your bad attitude if you bail.

❏ b) bag your plans, and tell your friends you'll make it up to them later, on a day when you don't feel like reheated pepperoni.

❏ c) go with your buds and order up a slice with everything on it. You listen to them gab but don't bring up your bad day.

No way or Yes way?

____6. Do you think any of your friends have ever lied to you about something major?

____7. Have you ever confronted a friend about something she does to you that drives you nuts, but she still didn't quit?

____8. Have any of your friends ever teased you so much about something you wanted to do that you backed out 'cause it wasn't "cool"?

____9. Has anyone ever tried to convince you that one of your friends has a bad rep?

____10. Do you sometimes feel uncomfortable being your silly self around your friends?

Check all that apply:

____11. You could imagine one of your friends doing something she felt was wrong, just to be in with the right crowd.

____12. Your secrets aren't always super safe when you share them with your friends.

____13. Lots of other peoples' secrets aren't safe with your friends. You know the lowdown on everybody!

____14. Your friends criticize other people all the time.

____15. Lies and exaggeration are normal to your friends, even if it means someone gets hurt.

____16. You and your friends are ultraclose. If you became friends with someone outside your posse, they'd be upset.

____17. Sometimes you feel like all your free time is zapped away doing things your friends want to do.

____18. At least one of your friends has a long list of enemies.

____19. Once in a while you get a creepy feeling that your friend is hiding something from you.

____20. If you admitted you had a crush on hotguy, you'd be afraid that one of your friends might tell him, or worse, go after him!

____21. Your friends' thoughts and feelings always seem to come before yours. Your thoughts and feelings rarely get priority.

____22. Saying no to your friends is sometimes scary. You want them to like you.

____23. You wish your friends would listen to you more. They can be kind of flighty and aren't always there when you need them.

SCORING

Are you choosing great friends or duds? Add up your score,
and read on.

1. a) 2   b) 3   c) 1
2. a) 2   b) 3   c) 1
3. a) 3   b) 2   c) 1
4. a) 2   b) 1   c) 3
5. a) 3   b) 1   c) 2

6 through 10:
Add 3 points for each yes; 1 point for each no.

11 through 23:
Give yourself 3 points for each statement you checked.

SMOOTH SAILING　　　　　　　10 TO 30 POINTS

Can we have your friends? They seem like the most
trustworthy buds around. The best friends to have are ones that
let you be yourself and also challenge you to grow as a person.
You know that sometimes friends'll let you down or disappoint
you, and you may do the same, but over the long haul, you're
there to support each other. Continue to follow your intuition
and your feelings. When you have friends who make you feel
safe, comfortable, and loved, you have friends with staying
power.

MURKY WATERS　　　　　　　31 TO 49 POINTS

Don't label a friend untrustworthy after just one or two
mistakes—nobody's perfect all the time. But if you've been
burned more than that, a warning bell should be going off! Are
you giving all the time—and getting nothing in return? Trust-
buster alert! Also, can you be yourself with her? If you put up
an act when you're with her, she's not right for you. There are

zillions of people in this world you can have loads of fun with—and who'll make you feel like the fabulous person you are.

SWIMMING WITH SHARKS   <u>50 TO 69 POINTS</u>

Sacrificing all your wants and needs to make your buds happy? Herbert L. Gravitz and Julie D. Bowden, authors of *Recovery*, say that you need to develop your intuition with tiny steps, so you can figure out whether you can trust someone. Share a little piece of you with a friend, and then check out her reaction. If you feel good, she's probably being supportive and trustworthy. Go on and trust her with another piece of you. Just remember: A true friend will like you for who you are—faults and all.

Are You a Spender or a Saver?

What do you do with your dough? Are you deeply in debt or laughing all the way to the bank?

1 Your bank balance is:

❑ a) under $10.

❑ b) about $50.

❑ c) in the hundreds.

2 The parents you're sitting for give you a major bonus for being so nice to their spoiled sweetie. You:

❑ a) go out and splurge. The money is burning a hole in your pocket.

❑ b) catch a movie and save the rest for a rainy day.

❑ c) put it all in the bank. You're getting 10 percent interest on your student account.

3 You're throwing your best bud a surprise party, and it's gonna be a major event. Do you:

❑ a) hit the gourmet grocery stores—only the finest for your friends?

❑ b) stock up on chips, dip, and soda at the local buy-in-bulk?

❏ c) ask everyone to bring something? Your pals get the major munchies, and it would cost you a fortune to feed this hungry bunch.

4 You're broke, but the new Jewel CD just came out and you've gotta have it. You:

❏ a) break into your piggy bank and hope the record store cashier won't mind the pennies, nickels, and dimes.

❏ b) give the house a makeover (you even scrub the tub) and ask Mom for an advance on your allowance.

❏ c) wait for a friend to buy it so you can tape her copy.

5 You're supposed to be saving for a class trip, but you really need a dress for the winter dance. You:

❏ a) hope Mom and Dad will pick up the tab for your class trip (it's an educational expense, right?) and spend your savings on a to-die-for dress.

❏ b) hit the bargain-basement stores. You love hunting for discount duds.

❏ c) pick something off the rack—the one in your bedroom closet, that is.

6 When it comes to an allowance, your parents:

❏ a) give you money when you need it—and that's, like, almost every day.

❏ b) put half in your savings account, then you spend, spend, spend the rest.

❏ c) hand it over. You're the financial wizard in the family.

7 It's Friday night, and your friends want to grab some pizza. You:

❏ a) try to convince them to go for something a little classier.

❏ b) love to pig out on pies, especially the extra-large vegetarian.

❏ c) tell them you've got tons of fixings in the fridge, so why not eat in?

8 The last couple of times you went to the mall, you:

❏ a) bought whatever caught your eye.

❏ b) had something specific in mind.

❏ c) didn't buy anything at all.

9 For your birthday, Grandma buys you a cellular phone—and she'll pay the monthly bill! You:

❏ a) go for the super-duper digital model, complete with built-in answering machine. Sky's the limit when Granny's buying.

❏ b) comparison shop. You hate to pay more than you need to, even if it's not your money.

❏ c) ask if she'll pay for a line to be installed in your room instead; you've heard horror stories about how expensive calling on cellular phones can be.

10 What best describes your personal philosophy when it comes to cold, hard cash?

❏ a) Cuba Gooding, Jr., said it best: "Show me the money!"

❏ b) Money can't buy happiness.

❏ c) A penny saved is a penny earned.

11 Your best friend offers to get you a job at the juice store where she works. You:

❏ a) say "Thanks, but no thanks." Mom and Dad pay for everything, so why bother blending for a living?

❏ b) jump at the chance. A little extra cash will come in handy with Christmas just around the corner, plus it's all the free smoothies you can drink.

❏ c) have so many other money-making schemes going on (baby-sitting, mowing lawns, walking dogs) that you don't have time.

SCORING

Time to ring up the register: $1 for every time you answered A, $2 for every B, and $3 for every C.

BIG SPENDER $11 TO $16

You're financially out of control, and it's gonna get you in trouble. Sure, it might seem like no big deal right now (especially if Mom and Dad are bankrolling your spending spree), but at some point you will want or need something important and won't have the money to get it, says Tracy Howard, a financial consultant in New York City.

Since your expenses are pretty low right now (we're talking no rent or car payments), this would be a good time to start a savings plan. If you've got a job, put away at least half of your salary. That way, when an emergency comes up, you'll have the cash to cover it. If you depend on the folks for a weekly allowance, tell them you'd like to put some of it aside in a student savings account at the local bank. Mom and Dad will be impressed by your new money-management skills—they might even raise your allowance!

DISCOUNT DIVA $17 to $26

You won't buy a pizza unless there's a two-for-one special, and you only go to the movies on half-price night. But you've realized that being on a budget doesn't mean you can't have fun. When something truly important comes along, you're up for the ride. Sure, it might set your savings account back a little bit, but you can't put a dollar amount on bonding with your buds. Besides, you're hip to the best bargains in town, whether you're going out for an affordable dinner date or buying party supplies on sale. Just make sure you're not spending more than you should to get a good bargain. Say you snagged a shirt for practically nothing at a designer discount outlet. Did you really need it, or were you just dazzled by a deal? Resist. Then you'll really start saving money.

PENNY PINCHER $27 to $33

You get an A for saving but an F for spending. We'd like to congratulate you for sticking to your budget, but we're afraid you're doing it at the expense of living. Like, when was the last time you treated your best bud to lunch?

Your stingy ways are also making you miss out on memorable experiences. You say dinner with friends is too expensive, but it's not 'cause you don't have the cash. You just can't stand to spend it. There's nothing wrong with wanting to save your money, as long as you're not living like a hermit to do it.

"I was a saver," says Howard. "But even when I had lots of money, I couldn't enjoy myself, 'cause I kept thinking I was going to need this money for something else." So set a small sum of mad money aside, and forget the financial strategies.

Do You Act Your Age?

Act your age—not your shoe size. Unless you're Dennis Rodman or some other feet-the-size-of-China type, that may be easier than it sounds. So, how are you hangin' on the numbers scale? Take this quiz to find out.

Read each scenario and write down whether it applies to you most of the time (M), sometimes (S), or never (N).

_____ 1. When a friend has a problem, she usually comes to you for advice, and most of the time, she does what you suggest.

_____ 2. On the day report cards are sent home, there's not a bead of sweat to be found on your brow. You're totally confident you did your best and that your grades will reflect that effort.

_____ 3. When a friend has a secret, she knows she can trust you not to squeal—not even to your best bud (and not even if it's a really, really good secret).

_____ 4. You've been in trouble for disrupting class.

_____ 5. Your parents sound like a broken record—or a skipping CD—asking you a zillion times to do your chores before you actually pick up a broom.

_____ 6. You follow the news closely and know what's going on in the world.

_____ 7. When you hear someone is talking bad about you, you talk bad about her behind her back to anyone who will listen.

_____8. You take time out to volunteer with an organization that could use your help—and you stick with it.

_____9. In the past year or two, your parents have started getting in your face less. You think it's because they've started trusting you more.

_____10. You don't care what other people think about your clothes and how you dress. You aren't dressing for them anyway.

_____11. You have a hard time standing up for things you believe in.

_____12. If you found your sibling reading your diary, you would go ballistic and hit him or her.

_____13. You're good at holding on to friendships.

_____14. When you get into a fight with someone, it's hard to swallow your pride and be the first to apologize—even if you know it's entirely your fault.

_____15. Persistence, schmersistence! Unless a skill comes easily to you, you don't want to be bothered with it.

_____16. Everyone at school knows you're a better news source than CNN. Your locker is, like, gossip central.

_____17. You love hangin' with friends but can only enjoy it if you know your schoolwork is done.

_____18. You never forget your family's and friends' b-days and other important days.

_____19. You like to show off to your friends by pushing around people who aren't as popular as you are.

_____20. You don't like it when your parents tell you that you have to set an example for your siblings. Isn't that their job?

SCORING

Do you think you act your age? Find out if your scores agree.

1. M=3	S=2	N=1		11. M=1	S=2	N=3
2. M=3	S=2	N=1		12. M=1	S=2	N=3
3. M=3	S=2	N=1		13. M=3	S=2	N=1
4. M=1	S=2	N=3		14. M=1	S=2	N=3
5. M=1	S=2	N=3		15. M=1	S=2	N=3
6. M=3	S=2	N=1		16. M=1	S=2	N=3
7. M=1	S=2	N=3		17. M=3	S=2	N=1
8. M=3	S=2	N=1		18. M=3	S=2	N=1
9. M=3	S=2	N=1		19. M=1	S=2	N=3
10. M=3	S=2	N=1		20. M=1	S=2	N=3

BEHIND THE TIMES   20 TO 34 POINTS

You're reading this quiz, which is a sign that you want to grow up and act your age. But let's be honest—you're not quite there yet. It's fun to play pranks and hang out with friends when you should be studying or helping out at home—but it's also a bad idea to neglect school and responsibilities. "Part of growing up is being able to look at the future in a bigger picture," says Dr. Pat Hudson, a family therapist in Dallas and author of *The Solution-Oriented Woman*. The grades you make today and the way you conduct yourself all have a big impact on your future, like it or not. Another important part of growing up is being able to determine what's right and wrong. That means choosing not to harass the new sub in history class, skip your homework, or gossip about that chem teacher you don't like. "There are opportunities around you all the time to be a good person," says Hudson. Why not try to get to know the teacher (you might find out he or she is really cool) or help the new sub by taking roll for him since he won't know all of the students? "Usually, bad behavior comes from a person who isn't feeling too good about herself or her life," Hudson adds. So fix it!

GROWTH SPURT   35 TO 49 POINTS

You're on the road to maturity, but you've hit more than a few bumps along the way. Still, try not to obsess over little slipups—just make sure you recognize and learn from them. For starters, look over the questions again to see which ones you could've gotten a higher score on. Were they the questions dealing with school stuff? Or asserting your individuality? Maybe your relationships with friends or your treatment of other people is a weak area. Once you recognize where you need to improve, it's only a matter of time and determination before you're able to work it out. How 'bout keeping a list in your diary of things you did right and wrong, along with ideas on how to correct them next time around? That way you'll be able to track your growth. Don't worry—becoming a better, more mature person is something everyone is trying to do every day, no matter what her age!

LI'L MISS MATURITY   50 TO 60 POINTS

You definitely act your age, and you might even act your parents' age. You are a model for people everywhere. You not only know how to take responsibility for yourself and your future, but you're also one of the rare few who are able to look past their own wants and needs to see the needs of others. A lot of people might not understand how you can be so together, but give them time. They're wishing they could be more like you—or they will be in a few years when they've grown up and realized how valuable maturity is! One caution: In your race to conquer (and save) the world, make sure you still have time for fun. "A truly rounded, happy person is one who can get the job done but still get silly," Hudson says.

Do You Worry Too Much?

Got butterflies in your tummy? Spend nights tossing and turning, thinking about your probs? Take this quiz to see if you need to chill.

1 When you turned in that big algebra test today, you felt jazzed that you'd kicked some serious algebraic butt. But later tonight, you:

❏ a. second–guess the answers you gave on the test. By the time you go to bed, you're convinced you flunked.

❏ b. think about the test once or twice, kicking yourself over the few problems you might've screwed up.

❏ c. give yourself a pat on the back. You're still secure that you did okay on the test.

2 That expensive dress you begged Mom to buy you for the dance looked great when you got it home two weeks ago. When you try it on again the morning of the dance, you realize it fits kind of funny in the shoulders. You:

❏ a. burst into tears, worried that everyone will think you look like a linebacker. You beg Mom to take you back to the mall to buy something better—even though the dress can't be returned.

❏ b. have Mom drive you to the dry cleaner's and beg the seamstress to de-poof the poofy shoulders.

❏ c. raid your best bud's closet and find a sparkly,

sheer scarf to wear across the shoulders. The look is really glam, and you feel better.

3 The cutie you've gone out with a couple times stops calling, and you can't stop thinking about him. You:

❏ a. sit by the phone all week and obsess over whether it was something you said.

❏ b. keep listening for the phone to ring but go ahead and plan to see a movie with your buds.

❏ c. realize that he could be doing something intense, like studying for the SAT.

4 You were in a foul mood this morning, and when one of your best buds attempted to cheer you up, you snapped and told her to mind her own business. You:

❏ a. lie awake at night filled with guilt as you replay the spat in your mind. You're sure she'll never speak to you again.

❏ b. feel your stomach churning every time you see her in the halls. You make a point to avoid her for the rest of the day, hoping that by tomorrow, she'll cool off and forget about your comment.

❏ c. find her, take a deep breath, and apologize for your rude remark. You know that your friendship can survive your bad mood.

5 One of the girls in your group of buds has a party and doesn't invite you. You:

❏ a. freak and think that all your friends are dropping you.

❏ b. feel a little disappointed but find out that your best bud wasn't invited either.

❏ c. go on as if nothing happened; it's not the end of the world. Maybe it was just a simple mistake.

6 Your crush invites you to the movies, but the morning of your date, you wake up to find a huge zit doing a mean impersonation of a third eye in the middle of your forehead. You:

❏ a. call and cancel the date immediately because you're positive he wouldn't want to be seen in public with your freakish self.

❏ b. arrange your bangs over the spot and worry that he'll run the other way if your monstrosity reveals itself.

❏ c. slap some coverup on it, or wear a baseball cap. After all, it happens to everyone.

7 That sore throat that's been driving you batty means one thing: Say buh-bye to those tonsils. The doc says it's just a minor operation, but you:

❏ a. leave his office feeling doomed, positive that something will go wrong.

❏ b. are a little nervous about the procedure and have trouble falling asleep the night before the surgery.

❏ c. learn all you can about the operation and ask the doctor a ton of questions to reassure yourself.

8 To get a passing grade in your history class, you're required to give an oral report in front of the entire class. The idea scares you to death, so you:

❏ a. spend the week with your stomach in knots, then play sick that day. You'd rather take a bad grade than risk passing out in front of the class.

❏ b. feel a little jittery when it's your turn to get up in front of the class, but you manage to get through it—and only flub once or twice!

❏ c. prepare all week for the big day. No matter how badly it may go, you'll know you did your best.

SCORING

Give yourself 1 point for every A, 2 points for every B, and 3 points for every C.

FRANTIC AND FRAZZLED   8 TO 13 POINTS

Overboard worriers like you have vivid imaginations. Being creative is cool—but you see disaster around every corner, girl. "Worrying is natural," says Dr. Eve Mayer, Ph.D., a Scottsdale, Arizona, therapist. "But teens carry it too far. This makes for unhappiness and depression." Instead of fearing failure, keep busy. Volunteer, play a sport, or get a part-time job. You won't have time to waste worrying—and as a bonus, you'll feel totally satisfied with your accomplishments.

NERVOUS NELLIE   14 TO 19 POINTS

You don't sweat the small stuff like total worry junkies do, but you're not living a worry-free existence either. You stress over stuff that's not within your control today, like your future, college, and other big, scary issues. That kind of worry is normal—and healthy. Just don't keep it inside till you explode. "Discuss it with friends who may be going through the same problems," Mayer says. Don't bum over the past or worry about the future. Live for today.

OH-SO-CALM   20 TO 24 POINTS

Congratulations, Miss Levelheaded! You know you're strong and don't freak out about stuff you know you can handle. You probably feel pretty good about yourself, huh? Well, you should. "It's rare [for a teen to have] this level of sophistication," Mayer says. You've taken control of your life this far, and you accept it when there's a problem you're unable to fix. Congrats! That's called maturity. With this attitude, you'll make an awesome leader and problem-fixer.

4 SUREFIRE WAYS TO LESSEN YOUR STRESSIN'

— When worries strike, write 'em in a journal. Two weeks later, read your worries list and look for patterns in your behavior.

— Faced with a big decision? Write a list of pros and cons to help you figure out which decision is the more logical one.

— Exercise regularly. Worrying makes your body way tense.

— Talk your problem over with someone. You might get some pretty rockin' advice.

How's Your Body Image?

What's the skinny on your body image—great, good, or just plain gross?

1 Seconds before walking into science class, a pal tells you the hottie you've had a crush on for weeks is thinking about asking you out. You:

❏ a) feel sick and run to the bathroom to check your face and outfit. Who cares if you get into trouble for being late?

❏ b) feel queasy but stoked and force yourself to walk in while you stare at the ground.

❏ c) feel a little nervous but walk into class with your head held high.

2 You pop in your fave aerobics tape when you get home from school because:

❏ a) the only way you'll attract the hot guys is by having the perfect bod.

❏ b) you felt a little out of shape today and know that working out usually makes you feel better.

❏ c) you like the way you look, and you feel great after working out. You also know that regular exercise is terrific for your health.

3 You're cruising the mall with your best buds when you see that gorgeous guy you've had a crush on for weeks headed your way. Suddenly you

remember the monster zit on your cheek. You:

❏ a) duck into a store before he has time to see you.

❏ b) wave hello—while you're safely hidden from his view behind your friends.

❏ c) momentarily stress, then decide that if he's grossed out by a zit, he's a loser anyway. After all, everyone gets 'em.

4 Your dad forces the fam to watch home videos. When your face fills the screen, you:

❏ a) grind your teeth in embarrassment.

❏ b) feel a few butterflies, which pass as soon as your jerko big bro replaces you on the tube.

❏ c) laugh, since everyone looks goofy on video. Then ask Mom to pass the popcorn—you're starving.

5 You're buzzing through the mall when you accidentally bump into a Cameron Diaz clone. You:

❏ a) are totally green with envy and bump into her again.

❏ b) feel a little insecure, but it's no biggie.

❏ c) apologize because you ran into her, then walk away without a second thought.

6 The cutest guy in English class says you look totally stylin'. You:

❏ a) assume he's talking to the girl behind you and look over your shoulder to see what she's wearing.

❏ b) think you look pretty cute too, but you wonder if he's saying that so you'll do his homework for him.

❏ c) say thanks and know it's true 'cause you're feelin' it.

7 When you look in a mirror, you:

❏ a) always concentrate on what you don't like instead of what you do like.

❏ b) study your reflection—there are good points and bad points.

❏ c) smile because you're usually happy with what you see.

8 When pool season hits, you're:

❏ a) afraid to get in the water because it means shedding your T-shirt.

❏ b) comfortable shedding your T-shirt—but only if your best buds are poolside with you.

❏ c) first to strip down to your bikini. It's hot outside!

9 If you could change some things about your appearance, what would you pick?

❏ a) everything, because it's probably better to start from scratch.

❏ b) a few things but nothing major.

❏ c) maybe one thing, but you're pretty happy with yourself overall.

Total the number of answers you checked for each letter.
Then read the description that corresponds to the letter you
checked most often to find out how you see yourself.

IN CRITICAL CONDITION   MOSTLY AS

Okay, with all the changes going on in your bod, having a little
self-doubt is normal. But your body bummage is in overload!
"Teen years are the worst when it comes to having a negative
body image," says Sandra Tabbernnee, an Oklahoma City
counselor. When you catch yourself saying negative body stuff,
stop. Think of what you just said. Whether it's "I'm so fat" or
"I'm so flat" or some other harsh thing, ask yourself, "Would I
say something like that about my best friend?" No, you
wouldn't. So don't trash the person you should love and
support the most: yourself! Concentrate on moderate exercise
and eating right to give your confidence a boost. And the next
time you compare yourself to Sarah Michelle Gellar while you
worship at the altar of Buffy, use that remote to do something
it's rarely used for: Turn off the TV, go jogging, read a
magazine, or cruise the Net instead.

IN STABLE CONDITION   MOSTLY BS

Some days you feel totally up; others, totally down. What
seems like a humongous flaw one day is bearable the next.
Shakin' your groove thing (um, exercising) helps you deal with
bad days 'cause it makes you feel better inside—and outside.
"On days you're unhappy with your looks, ask yourself why,"
says Tabbernnee. "It's probably because you're comparing
yourself with an impossible ideal. The only truly important
thing is that you're healthy and you like yourself."

Translation: You don't have to be Brandy to be happy. Beauty comes in all shapes and sizes. Accentuate your good points—stop trying to be that perfect size four, and be happy with who you are. After all, there's no one else like you.

COOL & IN CONTROL   MOSTLY Cs

Instead of dwelling on what little things you'd like to change, you're happy with what you have. Your positive body image makes you happier and more confident—two very important traits. But when you do occasionally fall victim to an I-Hate-My-Body day, don't stress. "Everyone has some downtime now and then," Tabbernnee says. "Just remember that those feelings of insecurity will pass. Next time you're feeling down, try doing something active instead of looking in the mirror. It's a great way to beat the blues."

BOOKS TO LOOK FOR:

SchoolGirl: Young Women, Self-Esteem, and the Confidence Gap. Peggy Orenstein. New York: Doubleday, 1995.

The Body Project: An Intimate History of American Girls. Joan Jacobs Brumberg. New York: Random House, 1997.

Appearance Obsession: Learning to Love the Way You Look. Joni E. Johnston. Deerfield Beach, FL: Health Communications, 1993.

Your Body, Yourself: A Guide to Your Changing Body. Alison Bell and Lisa Rooney, M.D. Los Angeles: Lowell House, Rev. 1996.

THE CINDY CRAWFORD SYNDROME

Feel crummy when you're face-to-face with images of supermodels? Who doesn't! We've got some insider info to help you keep it in perspective: Those pics you see are majorly airbrushed and computer-sculpted to get rid of all the blemishes, hairs, whatever, that everyone has. The final picture may be sleek and zit-free—but the real person really isn't *that* perfect. So get wise, and don't compare yourself to someone who doesn't even exist!

Do You Give Good Advice?

Do friends track you down in the halls to ask for advice? If you're the Diva of Dilemmas, there's got to be a reason. Maybe you're a down-to-earth problem-solver with a knack for listening. Or maybe you're an egomaniac out to change the world to your way of thinking. Take this quiz to find out if you're the school guru.

1 Two good friends are in a gnarly catfight. You just get through giving advice to one when the other calls and wants your help too. You:

❏ a) calmly explain that you just got off the phone with the other friend. You apologize and let her know that you aren't willing to compromise your values by being disloyal and talking to both of them. She can't expect you to get stuck in the middle, can she?

❏ b) get as much dirt as you can from both—it's the only way to know the whole story. Besides, you don't want to show favorites or anything.

❏ c) tell her that you just got off the phone with the other friend—but let her know you're not taking sides. From there, it's up to her if she wants to talk to you.

2 When a guy pal asks for your opinion on a yucky situation in which a girl took total advantage of him, your honest first reaction is:

❏ a) totally rational. Emotion only gets in the way and makes it harder to find a solution to the problem.

❏ b) anger. How could anybody do something to upset such a great person?

❏ c) understanding. Feelings should be dealt with first. When he's cooled off, you can work together to hash out the best way to handle the situation.

3 You've been waiting all week for the next episode of *The X-Files*. Just as it's about to start, your friend calls in tears because she wasn't invited to the '70s disco party with all the trendoids at school. You:

❏ a) pop a tape into the VCR and record your show. You can watch it commercial-free once things have chilled out.

❏ b) politely interrupt her spaz attack and ask if you can call her back in an hour. After all, she'll still be there—Mulder and Scully won't.

❏ c) shut off the TV and give her your full attention. Plotting revenge takes 100 percent concentration.

4 Your best friend calls and asks for help. She just dented her mom's minivan while backing out of the garage—and she wasn't even supposed to have touched the keys. You:

❏ a) race over to her house with a hammer in your

backpack. You'll pound out the dent together before her mom gets home.

❏ b) calm her down and ask her to explain the details of the disaster. Then you work with her to figure out the smoothest way to break it to her mom.

❏ c) realize there's no way out of it and tell her so. She's going to have to accept her punishment and get over it.

5 A younger girl in the neighborhood swears you to secrecy and then asks your advice on how to handle a really scary family situation. You are unsure of what to do but decide to:

❏ a) tell her how you made it through a similar situation with your family or relate it to a movie you just saw.

❏ b) break your vow and tell an adult you trust about it. In this case, the girl's safety is more important than your word of honor.

❏ c) sit her down and explain that talking to you was the right idea but that she obviously needs a professional trained in the field—and you're definitely not that.

6 You and your best friend are hanging out at the mall when that really cute guy she's been drooling over from gym class walks up and asks her for some wardrobe advice. You're busting at the seams with a megahip suggestion, so you:

❏ a) put on a big smile and let it rip. It can't hurt to let him know what's on your mind—and besides, you're the one people usually ask for fashion advice anyway.

❑ b) put a cap on it and keep quiet. If he wants your opinion, he'll ask for it.

❑ c) let your friend offer her opinion first, then go ahead with yours, pointing out a couple of good examples on the racks and telling a real belly-buster of a funny story.

7 When a good friend comes to you and needs to talk about a problem, you always ask if she wants your advice before you dive in with your opinion.

❑ a) true   ❑ b) false

8 Before giving advice, it's important to:

❑ a) be a good listener and ask a lot of questions. Asking questions from many different viewpoints helps make difficult situations easier to handle—and helps people realize the right answer for themselves.

❑ b) inform the person with the problem that you refuse to hear anything other than the facts.

❑ c) let your friend know that you are on her side, no matter what.

9 A girl you barely know from the popular crowd tells you a juicy story involving other members of school royalty and wants to know what you think. You feel:

❏ a) superior and more than a little suspicious. Why would Her Highness of Hipness suddenly need your help—unless she recognized your brilliance or wanted something from you?

❏ b) totally stoked. You thrive on drama, scandal, and gossip—and can't wait to tell this cool girl exactly what you think about everything.

❏ c) flattered but a little uncomfortable too. You don't really know this person well enough to offer anything but the simplest advice.

10 On average, you're asked for your advice:

❏ a) by good friends when they're really bummed out.

❏ b) hardly ever. You try to surround yourself with the kind of people who don't advertise their personal problems.

❏ c) by many different people, about everything from their love lives to their hair color.

11 As long as you don't hog the show, it's okay to tell a friend if you've experienced problems similar to hers. This is true even if your decisions were bad ones. It lets her know you've been there and helps her trust you.

❏ a) true   ❏ b) false

SCORING

Add up your score below, then read on to rate your advice skills.

1.	a) 2	b) 3	c) 1		7.	a) 1	b) 3	
2.	a) 2	b) 3	c) 1		8.	a) 1	b) 2	c) 3
3.	a) 1	b) 3	c) 2		9.	a) 2	b) 3	c) 1
4.	a) 3	b) 1	c) 2		10.	a) 1	b) 2	c) 3
5.	a) 3	b) 2	c) 1		11.	a) 1	b) 3	
6.	a) 3	b) 1	c) 2					

GURU GIRL   11 TO 15 POINTS

Move over, Dear Abby—this girl's got the gift. You know what to say and when to say it. You listen, wait to be asked for your opinion, and don't try to force anyone into your way of thinking. You know your limits and when to seek outside help for really serious stuff. Your goal? To ask sensitive questions from as many different perspectives as possible. Nobody knows better than you that the best advice is to listen, to be positive, supportive, and encouraging, and to help a person find her own way out of a sticky situation.

TOO-COOL COUNSELOR   16 TO 23 POINTS

You're a problem-solver. Even before your friend has finished talking, you have selected the plan of attack for eliminating the problem. Go on, admit it. You kind of thrive on the drama of it all! As soon as the trouble is put right, you're tackling something else. Your ability to solve problems is super. Sometimes, though, people have problems that can't be solved right away—if at all. What's important then is listening. When you learn to hear what a friend is telling you, sometimes you find out that what's needed isn't an answer, but a question:

"How do you feel?" is one of the best to ask. It centers the conversation on the person's emotions and helps her talk out her feelings. It also shows you really care about the person you're talking to—not just what you're talking about.

DEAR GABBY   24 TO 33 POINTS

You're social, outgoing, and interested in everything happening around you. You've got lots of friends, and when one of them has a problem, you really take it to heart. In short, you're such a good friend that their problems often become your problems. Sure, it's important to share past personal experiences with your buddies—it lets them know you understand their problems. But no one should hog a conversation with stories about her life; it ends up sounding like a lecture. So before getting involved in a friend's dilemma, show some self-control and kick back in objectivity land. No more diving in headfirst! After all, your friend is counting on you to stay clear-headed, optimistic, and supportive, remember? After you've given it some careful thought—and only if it was asked for first—unleash those words of wisdom and good, solid advice.

Are You a Giver or a Taker?

Do you go after everything you can get, or do you give everything you've got (and then some!)? Take this quiz to find out how you score on the goodwill scale, then read on . . . you'll see that givers and takers have more in common than you might've believed.

1 You lent a friend your favorite CD over a month ago and want to get it back. When you ask her about it, she says she's still using it. You:

❑ a) tell her that's tough and get it back, *pronto,* then declare your CD library off-limits to her (even though you have been listening to her All Saints disc for the last two weeks).

❑ b) tell her no problem. You figure she'll return it when she finishes.

❑ c) suggest she make a tape of it, then return it.

2 Your mom has asked you and your brother to clean the garage while she's gone, but your bro decides he'd rather watch the NBA playoffs. You know that if the garage isn't done when Mom gets home, you're both in big trouble. You:

❑ a) do your fair share of the work and let him know he's in big-time trouble if he doesn't get the rest done.

❑ b) clean the whole garage.

❏ c) refuse to clean without his help, then get to your mom first with the bad news your brother created.

3 Your crush cancels your Saturday afternoon miniature golf plans because he says he's got an English report to finish. You find out that he was really shooting hoops with some friends all afternoon. What's your next move?

❏ a) Let's see how he likes it! You cancel your Thursday TV date because of a "school project" and go to the movies with friends.

❏ b) To err is human, to forgive divine. And after he explains how you're cutting into his time with friends, you feel even worse.

❏ c) See ya later, alligator. You explain how hurt you were, give him the opportunity to state his case, and see if he's truly sorry. If not, you give him the boot.

4 The parents of the kids you baby-sit call on Friday morning, desperate for help. They need you to watch the kids that night while they visit a sick uncle. Only problem is, the guy you adore is having a party that night and he's actually invited you—personally! You:

❏ a) can't disappoint them. After all, there will be other parties.

❏ b) tell them you have a previous offer and see if they can perhaps find another sitter. Tell them if they really can't find anyone, you'll break your plans.

❏ c) tell them that you have a party to go to. Maybe they can take the kids to the uncle's house.

5 You and your friends regularly lend each other money for things when one person is short on cash. If you had to "balance the books" and figure out who owes whom, you'd find that:

❑ a) you were all pretty much balanced out; you owed as much as you'd given.

❑ b) you had a hefty cash balance. You'd borrowed at least two-week's allowance and rarely loaned your dough.

❑ c) you were in the red. You feel like a loan shark after all the cash you have loaned out.

6 When you and your friends get into fights, you're the one who winds up calling to get things worked out.

❑ a) always true

❑ b) sometimes true

❑ c) never true

7 A guy you think is totally hot just asked you to the spring dance. Unfortunately, you're a little low on cash, and you know that your parents are having a hard time financially. When your mom, who's equally excited for you, says she really wants to take you shopping for a new dress, you:

❑ a) go and find a great dress that's not too expensive.

❑ b) tell her no. If you can't find something to wear that you already own, you'll just borrow from someone else—or not go at all.

❏ c) go and get the dress you've had your heart set on.
Even though it's costly, you figure if it makes you
happy, it'll make her happy.

8 Your friends know they can call you whenever
they have a problem, but it seems as though when
you call them with a problem, they're too busy or
preoccupied to listen.

❏ true   ❏ false

9 Friends never seem to remember your birthday,
even though you always remember theirs.

❏ true   ❏ false

10 When you're doing a group project at school,
you often wind up doing most of the work.

❏ true   ❏ false

SCORING

Add up your score below to find out where you fall on the
giving scale.

1. a) 1	b) 3	c) 2	5. a) 2	b) 1	c) 3
2. a) 2	b) 3	c) 1	6. a) 3	b) 2	c) 1
3. a) 1	b) 3	c) 2	7. a) 2	b) 3	c) 1
4. a) 3	b) 2	c) 1			

Questions 8 to 10: Give yourself 3 points for each true and
1 point for each false. Total your score and see if you're
giving more than you're getting.

THE PLEASER   30 TO 23 POINTS

Always anxious to please, you're an over-the-edge giver. But before you take credit for being totally selfless, listen up: This could mean you have a lack of self-esteem. "A giver does things because she's overly concerned about what others think of her," says Linda Eveleth, counselor of adolescents in Canyon County, California. "She feels the only way people are going to like her is if she does things for them."

This is especially true for teen girls, who are anxious to please and be accepted by others—usually by peers. To get out of this pleasing-pattern, take up a hobby or get involved in a sport that makes you feel good about yourself. Having your own interests helps you focus on satisfying yourself. Soon, you'll see that others are willing to give a little too!

A WELL-BALANCED DEAL   22 TO 16 POINTS

When you do a favor for someone, chances are you're not expecting anything in return. But guess what? Your friends and family are probably eager and willing to give back to you. Why? Because although you do things selflessly (not because you want something in return), you know how to accept a favor from others.

If you feel the balance move to one side or the other, take a closer look at the person doing the extra giving or taking. Let the giver know you like her even when she's not doing favors for you, and let the taker know you shouldn't always need to do things to prove your friendship's strong.

GIMME GIRL   15 TO 10 POINTS

Sounds like "Me first!" is your motto! You call on your friends when you're blue but disappear when they need a helping hand. Although some may be envious that you get what you want, what's underneath your behavior is the same thing that troubles the giver—lack of self-esteem. Eveleth says, "Because you're unsure of how others feel about you, you're constantly testing the water by seeing how much people will do for you."

Stop relying on what other people do for you as proof of their affection. A good first step is to give others your full attention. When you're on the phone with them, drop everything else— turn off the TV, close those magazines—and really listen. Next, give others your help. Try volunteering at a shelter or hospital. If your mom works full-time, give her some help around the house. You'll learn what they mean when they say giving is better than receiving.

How Well Do You Know Your Body?

Sorry, but watching a season of *ER* episodes doesn't necessarily make you a health expert. Since knowing your body is so totally important, take this quiz to see if you need to brush up on the bio basics.

1 Exercise won't help prevent cancer, but it will keep the heart healthy.

❏ true   ❏ false

2 It's better to wear any sunglasses outside than none at all.

❏ true   ❏ false

3 Men's immune systems are superior to women's.

❏ true   ❏ false

4 The average adult's brain weighs in at:

❏ a) 3 pounds.

❏ b) 6 pounds.

❏ c) 10 pounds.

5 Women cry more than men because they are more comfortable being emotional than men are.

❏ true   ❏ false

6 Nutrients are absorbed through the stomach to feed the body.

❏ true   ❏ false

7 The pancreas determines how tall you'll grow.

❏ true   ❏ false

8 Your diet should consist of ___ percent fat every day.

❏ a) 0

❏ b) 15

❏ c) 30

9 Once your eyesight begins to deteriorate, there's nothing you can do but get glasses or contacts.

❏ true   ❏ false

10 Which of the following are all parts of the body's immune system?

❏ a) fingernails, skin, antibodies

❏ b) nose hairs, mucus, skin

❏ c) stomach acid, mucus, saliva

11 Cramps are a fact of life. There's nothing you can do to prevent them.

❏ true   ❏ false

12 Blood enters the heart through veins.

❏ true   ❏ false

13 The body has ____ different muscles:

❏ a) 200

❏ b) 600

❏ c) 1,000

14 Smoking can severely damage the lungs.

❏ true   ❏ false

15 Getting sunburned now will increase your risk of developing skin cancer later.

❏ true   ❏ false

Answers

1. **False.** In addition to keeping the heart pumping strongly, exercise also prevents cancer. Studies of girls under eighteen revealed that those who exercised at least four hours a week had fewer incidents of cancer, especially cancer of the

breast. In the case of the reduction of breast cancer, researchers think it's because exercise delays the onset of menstruation.

2. **False.** Unless they block both UVA and UVB radiation, sunglasses can actually increase eyes' exposure to harmful rays. They do so by darkening the eye's "picture," forcing the iris to open wider, and allowing more exposure to the retina.

3. **False.** Women are thought to have better immune systems than men do, because of certain genes women possess for pregnancy.

4. **C.** Ten pounds.

5. **False.** Researchers say that the high levels of the hormone prolactin found in females is the cause. It produces fluid in the body, and girls have more of it than boys do. (In fact, until puberty, both sexes have the same amounts of prolactin, and that's why children of both sexes seem to cry the same amount.)

6. **False.** After going from the esophagus to the stomach, food enters the small intestine, where it is finally small enough to pass into the bloodstream in the form of tiny molecules. This entire process takes place in a tract 30 feet long.

7. **False.** The pituitary gland, located in the brain, controls growth.

8. **C.** Thirty percent of calories should be derived from fat, and like any vitamin or other nutrient, fat is essential to good health.

9. **False.** There are certain exercises that can be done to improve vision. Talk with your eye doctor to get more information, or see a physical therapist who specializes in

vision. Still, more than 50 percent of people in the United States wear either glasses or contacts.

10. **B.** Nose hairs, mucus, and skin are all a part of the body's line of attack against viruses and bacteria. If germs sneak by, other cells gear up to clean away debris. And if that doesn't work, antibodies appear to fight the flu or infection.

11. **False.** Exercising regularly, or at least when you feel crampy, eases discomfort. Eating a calcium-rich diet (or taking calcium supplements before your period) helps too.

12. **True.** Blood enters through the right side of the heart, which sends it to the lungs to receive oxygen. Then it goes to the left side of the heart, where it exits through arteries and eventually winds up in tiny capillaries. Through these arteries and capillaries, the body's cells are supplied with oxygen and nutrients.

13. **B.** Six hundred. Some muscles, like those in the arms and legs, have to be consciously moved, while others, like the heart, move involuntarily.

14. **True.** Okay, so this was a freebie. Everyone knows the hazards of smoking: extensive damage to the respiratory system, and a variety of cancers (among them cancers of the lung, bladder, kidney, larynx, mouth, stomach, and pancreas).

15. **True.** It's especially important to be protected by a high-SPF sunscreen (or even better, clothes and a hat) in the sun during your teen years, since 80 percent of average lifetime exposure to the sun (and the cell damage that comes from it) happens before age twenty.

Scoring

Give yourself 3 points for each correct answer.

0 TO 15 POINTS
How can you hang around with something so much and know so little about it? You probably know your crush's middle name and birthday, but not your body basics. Get to work!

18 TO 30 POINTS
You have some of the body basics down, but there's definitely room for improvement. When it comes to taking care of your body, what you don't know really can hurt you.

33 TO 45 POINTS
You're either a genius in bio class, or you're just interested in your body. Good for you! Practice all of the good-body stuff you know and you'll live a long, happy life!